Dancing Through Thistles in Bare Feet

Dancing Through Thistles in Bare Feet

A Pastoral Journey

GARY HARDER

Herald Press
Waterloo, Ontario
Scottdale, Pennsylvania

Library and Archives Canada Cataloguing in Publication
Harder, Gary, 1942-
    Dancing through thistles in bare feet : a pastoral journey / Gary
Harder.

    Includes bibliographical references.
    ISBN 978-0-8361-9386-2

    1. Harder, Gary, 1942- 2. Mennonites—Ontario—Clergy—
Biography. 3. Toronto United Mennonite Church—Biography.
4. Clergy—Ontario—Toronto—Biography. I. Title.
BX8143.H37A3 2007   289.7092   C2007-903785-2

To the five churches that have embraced my ministry—
Waters Mennonite, Yellow Creek Mennonite, Valleyview
Mennonite, First Mennonite, and Toronto United Mennonite—
and to the many, many people who have opened their lives to me.

CONTENTS

FOREWORD

Recently I was at a meeting where a former pastor of mine happened to be sitting at a table with me and a few colleagues. When I mentioned to the group that our tablemate had been my pastor some decades before, one of our colleagues joked, "Poor you!" The group erupted in laughter and then laughed again when my erstwhile shepherd asked, "Which one are you talking to?" Indeed, we'd been in church together more than half my life, and as the years pass, I grow in my appreciation of and empathy for those engaged in pastoral ministry.

I spend an awful lot of time thinking about pastors, and not just because I teach at a seminary. My whole life has been altered by priestly folk. I still remember fondly from my childhood the leaders I first heard preach, who invited me to consider ministry, who taught catechism, who oversaw worship, and who offered pastoral care. When I was a teenager beginning to think through faith and life issues, I often turned first to pastors with my toughest questions. It was a pastor more than anyone who taught me what it means to be an Anabaptist. To this day, I remain grateful week after week that my household and I are blessed by good pastoral oversight.

Along the way, I too became a pastor. For the first time, I saw the complexity of that bundle of tasks myself. One reason my tablemate and I could laugh at the joke about whom to pity was because years ago I had gone to him and apologized for some things I'd done and said when he was my pastor. "Now that I am a minister myself, I see and understand many things differently," I said. "I know better what you were dealing with at the time, and I can imagine how my attitudes and actions may have felt to you."

In the early days of my ministry, two decades ago, I met Gary Harder for the first time. I did not know much about this long and lanky fellow. But I did notice how he tipped his head to the side when he carefully listened to me, and I was impressed by the insightful questions he asked. I paid attention to him because of how he paid attention to me. As I grew into ministry, I discovered that my growth as a pastor happened most fruitfully under the influence, guidance, and example of other pastors. While I did not run into Gary regularly, I recognized him as a model and mentor worth emulating. When I saw him at a meeting or heard him speak at a conference gathering, I perked up my ears and learned.

Now as I help prepare pastors, I am interested to know what makes them tick, and I am curious about how to foster practices of pastoral ministry that sustain and enrich the church. I regularly recommend to my students that they learn from wiser, more experienced colleagues. Gary sometimes visits our school; he's been related to some of our students (as father, uncle, and in-law) and has taught here several times. We're always glad to see him when he comes. If he lived nearby, I'd work awfully hard for him to be around regularly. It is in meeting and getting to know excellent pastors that many experience the greatest growth in ministry.

This book is the story of a person who was surprised by a call to ministry (good pastors are often caught off guard by their calls). He loves his vocation, loves the churches he served (the last one for almost two decades), and was loved in the churches he served too. Everywhere he turned—his family, his congregations, the Scriptures—he saw God at work, often in startling ways.

As a person who loves order and careful theologizing, he also appreciates how God keeps moving beyond structures and institutions and doctrines. Some of the stories told herein are simple (plumbing problems, life on a farm) and others complex (families in crisis, churches in conflict). Gary shows honesty throughout, frankly sharing with us some of his own failures and shortcomings, including a major church conflict that went awry in the last years of his ministry.

Through it all, we come to learn of Gary's passion for Scripture texts that he calls both immensely life-giving and upsetting, his priorities and insights as a musician, his fondness for the farm life of his childhood and the urban gardening of his adulthood, and his love of Bach. We hear of his passions for ministry and outreach and of his sadness that the church often does so poorly at welcoming those that surrounding society writes off and rejects. We meet unforgettable characters from his ministry. And we keep seeing God at work and on the move.

Now that Gary is retiring, I don't expect we'll be able to have him at Associated Mennonite Biblical Seminary as much as I would like. But with his memoir *Dancing Through Thistles in Bare Feet: A Pastoral Journey* he and the generous congregation of Toronto United Mennonite Church (which gave him a sabbatical to do this writing) have ensured that we will still be able to benefit from wisdom learned and gleaned in more than forty years of exemplary ministry.

Arthur Paul Boers
Associated Mennonite Biblical Seminary
September 2007

PREFACE

My present location in life comes as a surprise to me. As I write this, I have retired from full-time ministry. Toronto United Mennonite Church, where I have been a pastor for nineteen years, gave me a wonderful gift—a five-month partial sabbatical, during which I wrote this manuscript. My assignment for those five months of January through May 2006 was to do some "reflective writing" in order to leave a "gift of words, perhaps a book" with the congregation on my retirement.

So here I am, trying to leave some thoughts that I hope will have relevance to more than a local readership. I am aware that words on a page may be a very small offering.

My whole journey into and through ministry still seems so improbable to me. Take my calling to the pastoral vocation in the first place. Either God enjoys using a sense of humor in choosing ministers or God isn't very good at it. I was particularly reluctant (and unsuited) to follow the call. Now, more than forty years later, I am reluctant again as I enter a new phase of life.

I keep on being surprised by the odd twists and turns ministry takes, by how much I have loved being a pastor and how much I have loved the congregations to whom I've ministered. I've loved it despite wrestling with my calling, with God, with myself, and with the congregations I served, and despite sometimes wounding others or being wounded.

This book is a reflection on the journey of a traditional pastor with a more-or-less orthodox theology seen through an Anabaptist-

Mennonite lens. Over the forty-two years in this vocation, traditional lines were fuzzy almost every day, and clean, straight perspectives kept blurring.

This book is personal and tells of my journey as a pastor, but it also tries to address some of the issues that the church has faced and continues to face. As the fruit of these ponderings, I've tried to weave together personal experiences with particular Bible stories and texts that seem relevant to them. It is a very human story, but it is also a sacred story because it embraces God's surprising presence and work.

As I began writing, I was surprised by how often I saw God at work in unexpected places, often in chaos. There were few or no answers to offer. Yet God worked in mysterious ways to bring healing.

By personality and training I am most comfortable working within the structures of the church and the routines of orthodox ministry. That is where I expect to see God at work. But as I reflected I became excited about those times when I saw God at work outside the order I try to live out. It helped me realize again that God cannot be contained by our structures or theology and will not be limited by our sense of order and our planning. That forced me to go to places where I am uncomfortable; I am writing about experiences that challenged me to the core.

So this book is filled with stories—mine, the church's, my ministry's. I've tried to create a lively conversation between experience and reflection through the lens of biblical texts relevant to the issues of our lives and the church.

I feel a deep gratitude to the five churches that have embraced my ministry and tolerated my idiosyncrasies. Waters Mennonite Church, near Sudbury, Ontario (1965-67), simply extended their love and forgiveness to this fledgling, raw, naive, untrained twenty-three-year-old directly out of college. Yellowcreek Mennonite Church, near Elkhart, Indiana (1967-69), continued training me and allowed me to test the ministerial waters as an assistant minister while I studied at Goshen College and Associated Mennonite Biblical Seminary. Valleyview Mennonite Church, London, Ontario

(1970-71), invited me to a year-long supervised pastoral internship that profoundly shaped my personal and pastoral identity. First Mennonite Church, Edmonton, Alberta (1972-1987), hired me straight from seminary and made an indelible mark on my pastoral identity and confidence. Toronto United Mennonite Church has been for almost twenty years, since 1987, my spiritual home and has loved me and pushed me to the edges of my capabilities. To all five churches I owe profound thanks.

I am deeply grateful to the many people who opened their lives to me as I tried to offer pastoral care. Their stories and those encounters, are sacred. I have shared some of those stories in this book, and that makes the story teller very vulnerable, especially because those moments have been colored by the lens through which I saw them. I have used pseudonyms for some people, but others have graciously given me permission to use their names. I tremble at the trust involved, and I pray that their stories will be received with a sacred respect.

I also thank the four "conversation partners" from Toronto United Mennonite Church who agreed to read what I wrote and to offer feedback: Marieke Meyer, Richard Ratzlaff, Michele Rizoli, and Lydia Harder. Early in this writing I was at a point of discouragement, even despair. I wanted to plan this manuscript carefully and logically, but it wasn't working. I shared my frustrations with them, and they advised me to write what was on my heart and about the passions that stirred me. That freed me to write, and I thank these partners.

Lydia Harder happens to be my wife and a theologian. From the beginnings of our relationship, we've been immeasurably enriched by our love for discussing, arguing, and debating theological issues and biblical interpretations. Lydia has always been my sharpest critic and staunchest supporter. She mercilessly cuts through the fog and shoddy generalizations. She explores new directions with me. She celebrates what I do and who I am, and she brings out the best in me. My deep thanks and my deep love to Lydia.

Gary Harder
November 2007

Chapter 1

CHAOS:

THE MESSY ART OF PASTORING

A broken toilet seat put me in a foul mood. My mood was so bad that our neighbor lady got wind of it and decided to come over to see if a pastor could really get into such a state. "This is something to see," she said.

My wife, Lydia, and I had planned an open house on Saturday evening for the good people of First Mennonite Church in Edmonton, Alberta. I was their pastor. But on Friday the toilet seat broke. Actually it was probably already cracked, but we only became concerned about it on Friday when I sat down and got a nasty pinch. I thought it would not be very hospitable to inflict that kind of pain on our guests, so I tried to fix it. But to tell this messy story properly, I need to go back further. It began with what was for me an ethical question.

During my first year as pastor of the church, a pleasant, eager, middle-aged couple had started to attend regularly. They fit into the congregation easily. I was so pleased.

Six months later I was absolutely shocked when they told me they wanted to get married, and they wanted me to officiate. It turned out that they had both been divorced, both had a number of children from their previous marriages, and now they were living together. That might not sound so shocking today, but it was in the early seventies. And it was not how it was supposed to be in the church. What should I do? The seminary didn't teach us about situations like this.

For advice, I went to the deacons of the church. We agreed

that it was better for them to be married than not married, and the deacons advised me to go ahead with the wedding. After all, the couple was—or rather, God was—in the process of transforming their lives. And through them God was transforming the lives of many of their extended family members. As I got to know their various offspring and nieces and nephews and brothers and sisters scattered throughout the province, I saw quite a lot of dysfunction and pain. But there was also healing going on. This couple, who knew divorce and common law living, were becoming an amazing spiritual center for the whole family system.

So I officiated that wedding. After that they regularly called to ask if I could help them through one crisis or another, or be involved in yet another celebration of some event in a family member's life. Over the years I married, buried, and counseled many of them, and prepared some of them for baptism.

On the Saturday afternoon before our open house, I was to officiate another nephew's wedding—out in the country on the back lawn of a farmhouse. It had been a very busy week, and I thought I had planned well. I'd met with the young couple a number of times to help them prepare for marriage and their wedding. We had talked about a number of issues, including the fact that they wanted to get married by a pastor but didn't really have much of a personal faith. We'd wrestled through these and other thorny issues. That was now behind us, and all I had to do was spend Friday evening and Saturday morning finishing my sermon and preparing for the wedding. No problem.

Then that toilet seat pinched my behind. And of course I had to fix it in time for the open house on Saturday evening. But if truth be told, I am not the world's handiest guy. In fact, I can get quite depressed just thinking about things that need to be fixed. Simply put, I'm a klutz when it comes to fixing anything. But I'm also stubborn. And I figured it shouldn't be too tough; all I had to do was buy a new toilet seat. Replacing the old seat looked simple enough at the plumbing store. I drove home confident that this job, at least, I could manage. Should take only a few minutes.

I set about removing the broken seat. Unfortunately the metal bolts that held it in place were rusted. I'm a strong man, and in my grim determination to wrestle off the nuts, the porcelain toilet bowl also broke, and water gushed all over the floor. Now what? Back to the plumbing store, this time for a whole new toilet, which I actually managed to install. But wouldn't you know it, the new one leaked too. It seemed to have a hairline fracture. I was convinced it came out of the box that way. But back at the plumbing store, the clerk was sure that I'd ruined it.

By then I was desperate. I called a hockey teammate who was a plumber. He agreed to come on Saturday morning, and by 12:30, we finally had a non-leaking toilet. But I had to leave immediately for the wedding, and with all my toilet woes I hadn't managed any preparation time at all. I would have to wing it. I was totally unprepared and empty inside, and depressed and angry to boot. I was in as rotten a mood as I ever get.

And it was raining. I raced forty miles to the farm, mumbling under my breath, a black cloud hovering over my brain. Some fifty people were squeezed into a farmhouse basement with a capacity of maybe twenty. The air was blue and heavy with smoke. Alcohol had flowed quite freely already, and one rather inebriated man kept making terribly inappropriate and crude comments throughout the service.

I prayed silently. "Lord, what have I gotten myself into? I don't want to be here. These folks aren't even church people. I feel lousy and I have nothing to offer them. I wish I could just disappear."

Then it happened, just when I least expected it. In that absolutely chaotic mess that encompassed both the people in the room and the pastor, the Spirit of God blew in, almost as if God said, "What possibilities for healing I see in this place! As long as the cranky pastor doesn't get in the way, I see endless opportunities for rebirth."

After the service I just wanted to get out of there. I felt like an empty shell. But people wanted to talk, and they didn't want superficial "nice service, pastor" small talk. They wanted in-depth engagement. One person was struggling with a drug addiction. Another's marriage was falling apart. A third person was suicidal. They all felt moved to talk to me because somehow God had mysteriously touched them that afternoon. They wanted to talk to me even though I hadn't prepared for the wedding properly, though I'd felt that I had nothing to offer, and though I had a heart touched with blackness.

Three hours later, I literally sang all the way home. My black mood had been replaced by an amazed joy. I arrived home just as the first guests came to the door for the open house.

I have often reflected on the larger scope of that story, which has profoundly shaped the framework of my ministry. What if I had refused to officiate the wedding of that middle-aged couple? What if I had insisted that I would have no part in condoning a sinful situation? What if clean lines and clear rules had won the day? I shudder to think of the immense obstacles I would have placed in God's way had I said no to them. I tremble to think that I could have aborted a healing, transforming journey for a number of people in those families.

The Spirit of God keeps working, often despite the pastor, and sometimes even through an empty, depressed one.

By the way, I mentioned my hockey teammate earlier. I played on a community "old timers" hockey team throughout my time of ministry in Edmonton (1972-1987). Few of my team mates went to church. I still play hockey once a week in Toronto. When I told my team that I was moving to Toronto, I learned how much they value pastors. They insisted they would make a trade and could get at least two lawyers and an electrician for their preacher. Why? you ask. Because it takes two lawyers to spew as much wind and one electrician to create as many sparks as one preacher.

The Chaos/Order Conflict

Pastoring, like loving, seems to be a messy art. One of the key attributes you need to cope with the ongoing mess is the ability to free yourself from ideas—whether self-imposed or church-imposed—of how things ought to be. I've learned that I must be ready to improvise. The problem is that I am, by disposition and personality, more of a straight-lines kind of a person. I like order, structure, and a planned, organized, predictable way of life. I like rules. Even my musical tastes and training are in classical mode, stuck to the immensely structured music of Bach and to reading notes on a page. Yet pastoral ministry is mostly done within more jazz-like improvisations.

And that terrifies me. Jazz doesn't go in a straight line. It's unruly at times, and you can't easily constrain it or write it down. You might hear a fine tune introduced, but then that theme becomes lost in obscure improvisation or modulation before again emerging in recognizable form. Each performance is a new creation, growing out of the creative impulses of the musicians. There is some structure of chord progressions and recognizable tunes—improvisation couldn't happen without it. But in the end, jazz at its best is an unpredictable and uncontrollable affair.

I take some comfort in knowing that Bach and Mozart were improvisers extraordinaire, and that Bach's music especially is often put into jazz mode today. I also take some comfort in the belief that my classical and orthodox training for ministry is a good foundation from which to improvise. But that doesn't make me comfortable when I don't have clear notation and when my daily pastoral experience demands spontaneity. I want all the notes already on the page in front of me before I start playing.

Most of my training prepared me to work within the frameworks of the church and within the boundaries of my tradition's Anabaptist and Mennonite theology, for which I am mostly grateful. I experience God at work through the comfortable routines and predictable assignments of my pastoral life. I expect God to work there. Otherwise, why be a pastor?

But what do I do with the confusion created by an unexpected crisis? What do I do with the unpredictable Spirit of God, who will never be confined to my sense of order, my sphere of ministry, or my understanding of theology?

I admire and even envy spontaneous people who are not bound to the constraints of time and planning, those people who act more freely than I can and who can improvise creatively around obstacles and through plans that go awry.

Mind you, within me are strong intuitive urges that give me joy in trying to be creative. This occasionally allows some innovative leaps of insight to emerge into my consciousness. It puts me in touch with my submerged perspectives and my spontaneous side.

But the structured and organized part of me is my true home. I like everything in my garden to be in neat rows, which allows for easy hoeing of weeds. But every once in a while, the intuitive part wants to let things emerge that can't be predicted or planned, to allow some colorful weeds. It wants to see new life and hope in the mess, confusion, pain, and chaos of life.

I identify with this anecdote by Eugene Peterson in his book *Under the Unpredictable Plant: An Exploration in Vocational Holiness* (Eerdmans, 1992):

> A group of seminarians I was once leading on retreat asked me what I liked best about being a pastor. I answered, "The mess." I don't think I had even thought it before. The answer surprised me as much as it did them. Sometimes a question does that, pulls an answer out of us that we didn't know was there, but the moment we hear it we know immediately it is exactly true, more true than if we had had a week to formulate an answer.
>
> Actually, I don't like the mess at all. I hate mess. I hate the uncertainty. I hate not knowing how long this is going to last, hate the unanswered questions, the limbo of confused and indecisive lives, the tangle of motives and emotions. What I love is the creativity. And what I know is that I can never be involved in creativity except by entering the mess.
>
> Mess is the precondition of creativity. The *tohu v'bohu* of Genesis 1:2. Chaos.
>
> Creativity is not neat. It is not orderly. When we are being creative we don't know what is going to happen next. When we are being creative a great deal of what we do is wrong. When we are being creative we are not efficient. (p. 163)

Almost every day my work gets messed up—and not just by small stuff like daily schedules routinely interrupted by urgent pastoral needs or well-crafted worship services that come apart at the seams because I forgot where I was in my notes. No, I'm talking about the bigger pastoral picture.

I live so much of my pastoral work in a gray zone where clear answers and clear perspectives and clear theology and clear ethics and clear morality aren't easily discernable. I wish I had simple answers to people's questions and problems, but I've found it just doesn't work that way. Real life all too often gets in the way. It seemed so simple in seminary. Yet in the real world people's injured lives aren't so easily operated on and sewn back together. Ambiguity replaces certainty. Sometimes I've had to admit that I don't have a simple answer—or no answer at all.

Continues Peterson, "Everything deeply human has at least an element of chaotic mess at the core" (p. 164).

An Interruption

While writing the above paragraphs, I received a phone call about Leo, an eighty-five-year-old stalwart of our congregation. He'd suffered a massive stroke and was in the intensive care unit of the hospital fighting for his life. And so it was time to stop waiting for words to come and instead to wait with a family for death to come.

Like most vigils, it was full of love and tears and prayers and farewells. It was a sacred time, amid the pain. Love was palpable, along with the presence of God in that exquisitely tender and yet also brutal suspension of time and eternity.

This vigil now makes my above paragraphs seem superficial. Yes, there was an interruption in my writing schedule, but that feels totally beside the point. It's true that a deathbed is not the place for clichés about giving comfort. How do I at that moment get in touch with the profounder depths of human love and loss, and with the profoundest mysteries of life and of death? Maybe only by being open to the Spirit of God and not by relying on my training or theology.

This vigil reminds me again why I love my calling, even when I'm helpless and silenced by the enormity of the mystery and pain of it. Even when I am newly afraid in the face of entering that space with a family. Even when I know it will evoke a great deal of grief in my own heart and I'll need comfort even as I try to offer it.

Leo brought joy to me in many ways, though he was at times a challenge. Probably no one in our congregation called me to account for my sermons as often as he did. He raised questions and affirmed specific points. He challenged and disagreed with other points. But, most often, some idea or issue triggered his memories and stimulated him about future possibilities. And then we would have a spirited discussion.

"Dad was a fighter," his two children said a number of times while reflecting on his life. "He had to be a fighter just to survive." Leo was a complex man; there were many sides to him, and different people experienced different parts of him. During World War II he was a soldier in the Russian army, conscripted against his will. His family called him a hero of the war. "He was not a war hero, but a hero of the war," they insisted. Even as a soldier Leo tried to save lives rather than take them. At one point in the war, the German army captured him and twelve of his men. He had learned German as a boy, so he could speak fluently with his captors, who had decided to shoot their prisoners. Leo himself had been seriously wounded and was almost at the point of death, but he pleaded for the release of his men. Not only that, he asked for advice about where they could hide to prevent recapture. The Germans agreed to both requests, but Leo remained with them as a wounded prisoner and later as a translator.

As battles raged around him, others raged within him. One was Leo's struggle for faith. Out of a kind of atheism, or at least agnosticism, emerged a deep, personal trust in God. His second struggle was with violence itself. In fact, he would say that his second major conversion was to pacifism and a conviction that Jesus' way is one of peace. These conversions, like all conversions, are far more complex than can be described in a few words. But to us at Toronto United Mennonite Church, Leo was a kind of peace hero, even though we knew him to be a fighter.

Peace was a big theme for him, as was flight after miraculous escapes from death. His emotions were complicated. There was a lot of pain inside, emotional scars that lodged along with the shrapnel he carried in his body. His relationships could be complex, as he sometimes projected his inner struggles onto them. There continued to be many battles for him to fight—emotionally, spiritually, and in his relationships.

Because Leo was orphaned and a refugee so early in life, the war essentially robbed him of his childhood. It was only in the last years of his life that he could reclaim some of that lost childhood through his grandchildren. I delighted to hear the stories of his love for them. He would try to teach them things on a university level when they were still only in grade school. Like many of us grandparents, Leo had more simple joy and fun and laughter with his grandchildren than he'd had with his own children. And he specifically requested that the children's hymn "Jesus Loves Me" be sung at his funeral.

In his last few years, Leo mellowed a bit. There he'd be, in the center of the sanctuary, earphones very visible on his head, listening intently to the sermon. As his hearing worsened, his singing got louder with a voice that even his family described as terrible. But he was more at peace with himself and in some of his relationships. He was able to step back and enjoy life and other people more. He'd also learned to affirm people even when he didn't fully agree with them.

I grieve the loss of this man whom I sometimes fought but always loved.

Mustard Seeds and All That Jazz

The interruption of Leo's vigil and funeral provides another window into the sacred. For life as a pastor, interruptions are routine; they are frequent opportunities to see something of God at work.

I confess that, for me, reading the Bible often feels like an interruption in my life and in my thinking. But here's what happens. I'll be looking for some clarity on an issue, say a model for marriage. Soon I discover that there isn't only one biblical model for marriage, but rather a number of them. The issue is far more complex than I thought it was.

Or, when I'm completely confident I know what a text means, I discover an alternate understanding. This happens especially when a passage is so familiar that I don't read it carefully anymore. Then something—another's comment, a commentary reflection, or even an intuitive leap that grows out of a forced reading—triggers a new insight and another, perhaps contradictory, understanding excites my imagination.

How can this be? Surely, stating "the Bible says" during a sermon gives us the authority to offer decisive clarity about truth and about what God wants of us. Just bow to the authority of the Bible and we will know God's will. Surely, there is no "mess" in our sacred Scriptures. But why then are there so many different ways we can interpret a particular text? If I gain a new insight, was my earlier understanding wrong? Is my new way the only right way? Are you always wrong if your interpretation is different from mine?

The parables of Jesus have something in common with jazz music, I think. They state a theme that's sometimes obscure in our cultural context. What do most of us know, for example, about sheep and shepherds? The texts don't provide enough information to offer a conclusive interpretation. The parables are often provocative, puzzling, insightful, perplexing, intriguing, and full of multiple meanings. Each interpreter, each preacher, improvises a larger piece out of the few notes provided, some with more skill than others.

The parables of the kingdom from Matthew 13 are like a "theme and variations" set. The basic theme is the kingdom of God. But there are a whole set of variations, each of which adds another coloring to what the kingdom of God is like. Perhaps it is like a field where wheat and weeds grow together. Or maybe it is like yeast that permeates a whole lump of dough. Or it could be like a treasure hidden in a field or like a pearl of great value or like a net full of fish. Each variation offers a new perspective, a new listening point for hearing what God's work on this earth is about.

The disciples of Jesus were hard-pressed to keep up with all the new syncopations and rhythms and out-of-the-blue(s) melodies. "Just give us the main point. Just tell us plain. Just stick to basics, Jesus. Tell us in a nutshell what the kingdom of God is like. What's with all these variations? Maybe we can memorize the main melody. Why do you keep on speaking in parables, Jesus?" But he replied in further poetic parable form.

> "The reason I speak to them in parables is that 'seeing they do not perceive, and hearing they do not listen, nor do they understand.' With them is fulfilled the prophecy

of Isaiah that says: 'You will indeed listen, but never understand, and you will indeed look, but never perceive. For this people's heart has grown dull, and their ears are hard of hearing, and they have shut their eyes; so that they might not look with their eyes, and listen with their ears, and understand with their heart and turn—and I would heal them.' But blessed are your eyes, for they see, and your ears, for they hear." (Matthew 13:13-16)

I can imagine that the disciples were still thoroughly perplexed by this answer. Parables keep falling around their ears. Tunes are spinning everywhere, and their straightforward question receives no straightforward answer that ends in a solid C major chord.

Some people, says Jesus, just won't look closely or can't listen carefully. They don't understand with the heart, because their hearts have grown dull. Any amount of clubbing them over the head with truth won't help. So Jesus speaks in parables, and to understand them requires imagination, wonder, surprise, intuitive leaps, and nonlinear thinking. All of which triggers a rush of new variations on the theme of the kingdom of God.

He put before them another parable: "The kingdom of God is like a mustard seed that someone took and sowed in his field; it is the smallest of all seeds, but when it has grown it is the greatest of shrubs and becomes a tree, so that the birds of the air come and make nests in its branches." (Matthew 13:31-32)

The message of this parable seems obvious. The kingdom of God started as the tiniest seed, with Jesus, and will grow into a triumphant, overwhelming tree that overpowers all other kingdoms of this world.

But wait a minute. Something doesn't compute. There are seeds far tinier than the mustard seed. And the grown shrub is a couple of feet high at most, not as tall as a tree. Is there a hidden theme somewhere, an improvisational tune ready to emerge?

Come to think of it, why didn't Jesus just use the image of a cedar tree instead of a mustard shrub if he wanted to say that the kingdom of God would start small and grow powerful? The cedar tree was already a very popular, almost mythical symbol for the Jewish people. We read about it in the prophesies of Ezekiel, who described a noble cedar. Every bird will come to nest there and find shade there, he said. But who are the birds? Likely Ezekiel was saying that the Gentile nations would be coming in subservience to the Jewish nation. Here the tree is a symbol of world domination (see Ezekiel 17:22-24; 31:1-18).

It was a member of our congregation who first oriented me to a new interpretation of this parable. Willi Braun was my friend and lay member of our preaching team. He was also a doctoral student in New Testament and challenged us to take a new look at this text. Quite discombobulating it was, challenging a simple interpretation held—and cherished—my whole life. And I have someone from my own church to blame for that.

Willi suggested that Jesus deliberately chose the symbol of the mustard shrub over the cedar tree for good reasons. Those listening to him would have immediately caught the contrast and the irony: the kingdom of God will not grow to world domination, as symbolized by the cedar tree. The kingdom will not demand allegiance or exert power like that. What then is the point of the parable? Why did Jesus talk about a mustard seed and say it was like the kingdom of God?

The mustard plant apparently is famous for two qualities. First, it is an uncontrollable, pesky plant. It grows wild without benefit of cultivation. In fact, in those days it was very hard to cultivate. The farmer in the parable who sowed it was obviously incompetent; once it's established, you can't get rid of it. Like the dandelion in our modern lawns, it asserted itself contrary to the farmer's wishes.

Is the kingdom of God like that? Religious leaders would have choked on this parable. You can't mingle classes of plants. That makes them unclean. Everything in the garden, in the synagogue, in life, has to be neatly separated, organized, orderly. Keep plants and people apart, pure, each with its own kind. Saints here, sinners there. Conservatives here, liberals there. Heterosexuals here, homosexuals there. God is a pure organizer. Above all, God loves order and regulation and neat rows with clear separations.

So why did God create the mustard seed (or the dandelion

seed for that matter), and why did Jesus use it in the parable to describe the kingdom? The plant is unruly, subversive. It mingles. It messes up. It is wild. It can't be tamed. It's like jazz music, refusing to fit the "proper" categories.

Truth to tell, I have a hard time fully embracing this interpretation emotionally. Even if God might like a world that tolerates chaos, I don't. I plant my garden in straight rows. I make lists. I like order. I am a classically trained musician.

But I also know deep down that the Spirit of God can never be tamed or controlled. I know that imposing my orderliness on the church would violate its spirit and soul. Deep down I felt a thrill of excitement while exploring this parable in this new way. The kingdom, Jesus said, is like a mustard seed—pesky, wild, uncontrollable, exasperating, subversive.

But there is more to learn about the mustard plant. In biblical times it was considered a medicinal plant. According to Willi's article on this parable, ["The Pesky Mustard Seed," July 10, 1993, *The Mennonite* (p. 10)].

> Variously prepared with other ingredients, mustard counteracted the poison of snakes, scorpions and fungi. It was a remedy for many ailments, including sore throats, toothaches, stomach troubles; it alleviated itch and leprous sores, scabrous cheeks, asthma, and dim vision, it revived those who had fainted, cleared the head and the senses. In short, people regarded the mustard as a cure-all.

Mustard was clearly a symbol of healing, which was one of Jesus' primary ministries. What a winsome image of God's kingdom! It sets my spirit loose to imagine an unruly and rambunctious sprouting of the Spirit moving and working beyond and outside our neat categories and theologies. Probably all churches (and most pastors?) are by nature inclined to weedless neat rows and hyper organizational gardening, especially Mennonite churches with their heritage of trying to be a pure church. But when we do that, we can sometimes miss the Spirit of God, who moves to a different rhythm, sings ever-new melodies, and explores even farfetched variations. The Spirit will never, ever be limited by our way of gardening. The

Spirit will bring together people we think should be kept apart and will mess up our interpretations and categories. The Spirit will do all that to bring healing to our world and to the church.

But I'm still not sure I'm entirely comfortable with mustard or dandelion images. I'm wild only occasionally and only in my imagination. So this parable of the kingdom both troubles me and excites me. I suspect that we all need some mustardy subversion that will allow a much greater flow of healing.

Another Vigil and a Spontaneous Wedding

About a dozen family members and close friends were gathered around a deathbed when we expected to be celebrating a wedding.

Jason had been diagnosed with cancer some years earlier. He had fought a number of battles that included several surgeries but had been in remission, and we had strong hope that he had been cured. He and his fiancée, Ingrid, had moved to Toronto from Vancouver and were preparing for their wedding.

Jason came to Toronto and into our lives acknowledging that he didn't have a personal faith in God. But God was working. Jason's suffering opened him to ask ultimate questions and to enter a spiritual journey. In the last several years of his life, he and Ingrid were drawn into a beautiful spiritual awakening. One of Jason's medical doctors was a sort of midwife to that birthing, offering prayer and hope along with expert medical care.

Jason and Ingrid took a faith exploration course I offered. Jason was on the quiet side but very involved intellectually and spiritually. He was alert and responsive to the issues we explored. Both he and Ingrid entered into spirited arguing and sharing as we explored basic faith issues and studied the world of our spiritual forebears, the sixteenth-century Anabaptists. The class members became very close, and we held a celebration party at the end of it.

At one point Jason requested a special prayer and healing service. So a group of family members and close friends gathered around him in his living room to pray for spiritual and physical healing as he entrusted his life fully to the love of God. Who knows whether prayer was a factor in Jason's extra two years of life, which were thought medically impossible.

Once Jason was in remission, he and Ingrid began planning their wedding. They wanted a Thanksgiving Sunday wedding service, and they wanted the theme of the service to be a celebration of life and love. They felt that *Thanksgiving* named what they wanted to express to each other and to God.

They both acknowledged deep pain and struggle over the last several years. There was the physical pain of the cancer and its treatments, and there was the emotional roller coaster of the raised and dashed hopes. Suffering had been a part of their growth as a couple.

One day I awaited their arrival in my office to begin marriage preparation and wedding planning. When they finally arrived, their faces said it all. They had just come from a visit with Jason's oncologist, and the cancer was back, this time with a vengeance, its fourth visitation in five years. Yet they still wanted to plan their wedding service. In fact, it seemed even more important, more urgent now, to have a wedding.

In a few days Jason was back in the hospital, and within a week we were holding vigil around his deathbed. How could anyone have known that their time together would be so short and so filled with an intense, powerful love.

That Saturday was a hard day for all those gathered in vigil, but there were some beautiful moments. Jason was fully alert and fully present, almost to the end. He fought hard to stay alive and alert until his parents and other family members could arrive from Vancouver. Later that afternoon he motioned that he wanted to give me a hug, and we embraced in a long, deep farewell. Particularly beautiful to me was the loving and exquisitely tender way in which Ingrid cared for him until the very end.

Jason had been in some anguish of spirit and asked us to pray for him. The prayer calmed him and gave him some peace. I felt a prompting in my own spirit to ask him, "Is there anything else you would still wish for before you die?"

Without hesitation, and with a bit of a smile, he said, "Yes, I would like to get married. My bride is here. Her family and my family are here. Our best man and bridesmaid are here. You are here. I would like to get married."

I thought, "Why not?" It wasn't planned, and I didn't have time to prepare this time either. We didn't even have a marriage license to sign. But the couple was ready with some spontaneous vows, I was ready to pronounce them husband and wife, and God was ready with an amazing blessing there around that deathbed.

The moment was absolutely sacred. The room was crowded with people—and with love. The wedding service was like no other I have ever experienced. The couple's poignant declarations of love for each other matched the traditional vows: "For better and for worse, in sickness and in health, till death do us part."

A short time later Jason slipped into unconsciousness and then into the arms of God.

Birthed Amid Chaos and Mess

One spring several years ago our backyard contained a striking combination of chaos and beauty. It was May, and the apple and pear trees were in full blossom, as were the lilacs and dozens of spring flowers. Aromas filled the air. As I awoke every morning, a choir of birds greeted me. The greening and budding and blooming of the earth had been unleashed; it could not be held back, contained, or controlled.

But our back yard was also in a state of absolute chaos, only a very minor part of which came from the fact that we hadn't gotten around to weed-control duty yet. Some of the flowers (mostly the yellow ones) weren't really supposed to be there.

The major part of the chaos resulted from the backhoe that had invaded our backyard. We were making a modest addition to our modest house, mostly for the sake of our grandchildren, and it seems you can't create an addition without some chaos. The backhoe dug trenches everywhere. Dirt piles lay all over the yard. What a mess! But our grandkids loved it.

The backhoe even dug through my cherished garden plot. I had been composting that spot into vibrant health for fourteen years. Our brick patio was torn up, and our best apple tree was now lopsided because I had to cut off the big branches on one side to make room for that digging machine. So our apple tree now matches our small pear tree, which has branches growing only toward the south. All its north branches had been torn off by grandkids, who thought they made great swords. Apparently we hadn't started teaching them our peace theology soon enough. Our abundantly producing grape vine was torn out by its roots, though supposedly transplanted elsewhere by the backhoe guy. And the fence protecting our backyard privacy lay scattered across the mud piles.

As I've said, I hate mess. Strangely, though, I really do like dirt. I have always enjoyed it. Inside of me beats a farmer's heart. Sometimes I still get nostalgic for my home farm in Rosemary, Alberta. It was an irrigated farm, and we were always digging in the dirt. My hands still like to work in soil, even when they don't have to. I can't seem to stop my hands from scooping up the soil to enjoy its textures and smells and to marvel at the life it contains.

But I really don't like to have dirt tracked into the house. Lydia likes it even less than I do. The house is to be clean, sanitized, pure. But when you have dirt piles in the backyard, some of it inevitably gets inside by way of shoes, hands, and clothing. Or the grandkids lug gobs of it into the house, and we go into a cleaning frenzy.

It helped when we finally poured cement over our crawl-space dirt, which became neat, clean, and covered over. All sterile once more, but with no life there.

As a pastor I often get dirt on my hands, walk where it's muddy, and don't know how to keep boundaries between outside and inside intact. There's life in the dirt, God's life, but I don't want to track it in to where I live. It's easier to keep it out, or cement over it.

Beauty and chaos continue to coexist in our backyard, though the mud piles are gone. But our grandchildren keep on digging new ones. They too love digging in the dirt, and they take great delight in creating deep holes where potatoes are supposed to be growing.

I suppose beauty and chaos will also continue to coexist in the church.

My Perfect Church

Occasionally the church and its ministers respond spontaneously to the challenges that come their way. But institutions tend toward inertia resulting from structure, planning, predictability, and self-preservation. They resist any hint of chaos.

"But not if I can help it," I mutter. And I set out to create the perfect church. I start with music. In my ideal church we would welcome people who like only classical music, so that we would hear only Bach every Sunday morning—hymns, worship music, choir, offertory, prelude and postlude, all by Johann Sebastian.

But this would cause a problem with one of my colleagues and close friends from an earlier ministry. He is now a long-distance trucker, as he takes a break from ministry, and that has corrupted his musical tastes no end: he's into country western. When I want to hum "Jesu Joy of Man's Desiring," he's ready to belt out "These Boots Are Made for Walkin'." So it wouldn't do to have him in my perfect church.

Next we come to how we would welcome guests in the ideal church. Certainly not the way we do in the church where I pastor. I suppose there are probably some folks who actually like to be introduced publicly, made to stand up, and state their name with all eyes on them. I've heard that there actually are some who enjoy that kind of thing and really feel welcomed when it happens. But the perfect church would be for people like me, who want to blend in with the woodwork, take their time to sort things out, and maybe then meet one or two friendly people at most, as long as there's time enough to sneak out before coffee hour begins. No, my ideal church would not have any public introduction of visitors.

I'm time-conscious, so at 9:55 a.m. we'd lock the doors so that everyone has time to get into their seats so as not to disturb the start of service at ten sharp. No latecomers and dalliers allowed in my perfect church—or loud people either.

Then there's decision making. Say, for example, we have to decide how to spend estate money. . . .

I'm shoveling as hard as I can, and still there is mess. I haven't even touched on things like theology and how to interpret the Bible and how we understand our heritage and whether to write out our prayers. I actually got bored just writing about my perfect church. I can't imagine a more lifeless and sterile place.

I Blame Jesus and the Holy Spirit for a Dirty Church

Jesus started the problem of dirt in the church with the people he chose to be his followers. He should have known better. He should have known that if you want a group to click, you get like-minded people together, all from the same class and ethnic background, with the same education, beliefs, and prejudices.

Jesus started his recruitment program on a reasonable note. He chose some fishermen. They wouldn't be my first choice, of course, but surely Jesus can choose from any group he wants. But he should have stayed with them. Instead, he next chose Levi, a tax collector, escalating the tension. After all, tax collectors were collaborators with Rome. They took taxes from folk like fishermen. Fishermen despised them; they knew that all tax collectors are cheats and thieves.

Then, if that wasn't bad enough, Jesus invited James and John, sons of Zebedee, to join their disciple group. Their nickname was "Sons of Thunder," which probably meant they were Zealots. Zealots liked to go around sticking their *sicari* (hidden daggers) into unwary Romans and their collaborators—people like Levi. Then there were all the others Jesus called, each of them characters—people like Peter, Judas, Andrew, and Philip, none of whom would win a Mr. Congeniality prize, each of whom had enough rough edges to capsize a fishing boat.

There were also the women—rich and poor women, who didn't know or wouldn't keep their assigned social place, who wanted to be friends, not servants.

Such an assortment of sinners would make one scream with discomfort.

I can't imagine a poorer choice of people to build a movement around. At the end they ignored Jesus' words about suffering and death, arguing with each other about who deserved the most prestige in Jesus' new world order. Who would be prime minister? Who would be minister of this or that? The only thing they had in common was that they loved Jesus. The only thing that united them was their commitment to following him. But was that really enough?

I think the Holy Spirit should share the blame too. Can you imagine a messier scenario than the one played out on Pentecost (see Acts 2). It was so chaotic and the disciples acted so strangely that some people taunted them for being drunk. You just can't mix people from different countries, who speak different languages, and expect them to get along. It's a sociological impossibility. But try telling that to the Holy Spirit.

The narrative seems so straightforward in describing that event on the day of Pentecost:

> They were all together in one place. And suddenly from heaven there came a sound like the rush of a violent wind, and it filled the entire house where they were sitting. Divided tongues, as of fire, appeared among them, and a tongue rested on each of them. All of them were filled with the Holy Spirit and began to speak in other languages, as the Spirit gave them ability. (Acts 2:1-4)

How incredibly chaotic! The text lists people from sixteen nations (see Acts 2:8-11), all speaking different languages, in that group touched by the Holy Spirit. In their own languages they heard the Galilean disciples "'speaking about God's deeds of power.' All were amazed and perplexed, saying to one another, 'What does this mean?' But others sneered and said, 'They are filled with new wine'" (verses 11-13).

It wasn't long before three thousand were baptized. This impossible mix of people started visiting and eating together, meeting in homes, praying with each other, and generally behaving as though they were one big family. Some of them even sold some of their possessions to help the poorest among them. And they couldn't seem to stop themselves from praising God.

We might have known that conflict was inevitable. Soon there was grumbling and complaints from the back benches. It seems that some of the Greek-speaking widows, the real foreigners, weren't getting their fair share of the soup and the bread. They were being overlooked in the distribution. So the Greeks complained. But then the disciples, the leaders, did a surprising thing. They invited those Greek-speaking foreigners to take on leadership responsibilities and authorized them to take care of the problem themselves. They did this by choosing seven of their own

Greek men to lead the food distribution in an equitable way. The disciples gave up some of their own power and brought the outsiders into leadership with them.

Where would it all end? It won't ever end. Not until the Gentiles too are part of the church. Not until the church spreads to every nation and every culture. Not until our worst enemy is invited in. Not until God's will is done fully on earth as it is in heaven. The chaos just keeps escalating.

It was much simpler for me to pastor a church of staunch German/Russian Mennonite background than to pastor the urban church I do now. I could try to stay in control and keep the church relatively "clean." We all spoke Low German and sang the beloved German *Kern Lieder* (literally "core" songs, the German Mennonite folk-like hymns which were at the heart of our hymnody). We knew what each other thought, and we had last names we could remember—and pronounce!—and we laughed at "in jokes."

But now we hear other languages sometimes and have to learn strange-sounding names. We see people who don't look at all Dutch or Swiss, or have white skin even. Sometimes we have to try to keep up with those lively Spanish songs—amplified yet. We listen as people celebrate their faith heritage from other denominational traditions. Because we have a refugee center in our building, a steady stream of "foreigners" comes through our church doors every day of the week. And so we hear gut-wrenching stories from around the world.

It just isn't quiet and peaceful anymore. Or simple. Or "clean."

We try to close the doors sometimes, but the Holy Spirit opens the windows and invites people who aren't at all like us into our lives, our hearts, our homes, our inner circles, as if differences and conflict aren't supposed to keep us apart. Faith in Jesus Christ is supposed to be a glue to hold us all together.

An irritating wind from God keeps blowing and is totally out of our control. When the church doesn't close the doors and windows fast enough, it becomes a cauldron of creativity, a place of fertile imagination, where new relationships are born and new solutions to insolvable problems are attempted. It is a very beautiful thing, even in the midst of constant chaos.

What About "the Others"?

Life is as good as it gets on the farm when the harvest is in. Wheat yielded fifty-seven bushels an acre that year, 1961. Irrigation and a hot summer sun had worked their magic. Nineteen-year-old muscles bulged from the irrigating, the haying, and the shoveling of truckloads of wheat and barley into the grain auger. The itchy barley dust that torments the skin was soon forgotten. The old International Harvester combine, so prone to breakdown, had somehow made it through another harvest.

I loved fall and felt close to the earth then. It was so satisfying to see our hard work, multiplied by God's bounty, richly rewarded with full granaries. Hunting season opened on Thanksgiving Monday. With a shotgun on my back, a friend at my side, a dog to point up the pheasants, we'd walk for miles in the warm October sun and end the day, hopefully, with a meal of roast pheasant. Life was good.

But fissures were working their way through my soul. My carefully crafted, premodern framework of life and faith was coming apart at the seams. Chaos was threatening.

We Mennonites were inclined to live in closed communities, easily separated from "the world." The world was sinful and evil. We remained righteous as long as we didn't allow ourselves to be contaminated by that world. We spoke German, "God's language," and called everyone else "the English."

But in Rosemary, Alberta, we had unusual neighbors. They were so unusual that I have not heard of another village community that brought together such a fascinating ethnic and religious mix of people. Rosemary was almost equal mixtures of Mennonites, Mormons, and Buddhists, though the Buddhists were in the minority. Our small village featured a Mormon temple, a Buddhist temple, and a Mennonite church.

As part of a deal in 1881 with the federal government to build a cross-Canada railway Canadian Pacific Railway (CPR) obtained a good deal of farmland along its right of way. The CPR needed to sell that land to farmers in order to fill its grain cars, so it built an irrigation dam on the Bow River near Bassano, Alberta, which provided water for the farming around Rosemary, making land there very attractive. The Mormons migrated north from Utah, through Alberta, in the early twentieth century to find farmland. We Mennonites came to Rosemary in the late 1920s and in the thirties as refugees from Russia. After World War II, the Japanese Buddhists came from British Columbia, where they had been interned by the Canadian government during that war.

So I grew up with Buddhist and Mormon classmates and friends, though it was always clear when it came to matters of faith that "we were right and they were wrong." But strange things happen when you live together, like the development of an unwritten and unstated understanding that we would not try to proselytize each other. It wouldn't work anyway, because each group had a strong identity, mixed with a great deal of stubborn pride. So we began to appreciate each other.

I had many theological arguments with my Mormon classmates. We were always trying to prove each other wrong. We had enough of a common knowledge of the Christian faith and the Bible to argue, as long as the Mormons didn't try to trump us with the Book of Mormon. In many ways the kind of dialogue we engaged in then was foolish; each side sought to attack the worst of the other side and counter with the best of its own.

I mostly remember these arguments as enjoyable and grudgingly respectful, but they were not always friendly. In the fourth grade a particularly vicious fistfight broke out in the playground during recess between two combatants, one insisting that God was a Mormon and the other just as vociferously insisting that God was indeed a Mennonite. I was only a bystander, but it was clear where my sympathies were.

The "problem" was that I became good friends with some of these classmates and came to respect them. Their lifestyle was clearly as "righteous" as was mine. Living our faith was very important to us Mennonites. While the Mormons did dance, and dancing was clearly sinful, in most other ways they were decent enough. We teased them for not drinking coffee or tea, forbidden to them because of the caffeine.

Then several of my classmates, firstborn sons, prepared to go on two-year missions for the Mormon church. That really impressed me. I could brag a bit that our Pax program under Mennonite

Central Committee asked for a three-year overseas commitment for young adults who volunteered, but I wasn't about to sign up.

I don't remember any such arguments with my Buddhist friends. We didn't have enough in common religiously to find a place to argue into. But I made some memorable human connections. My friend Keyoshi invited me to go along with his family to Calgary to attend a football game with my beloved Calgary Stampeders. It was my first professional football game and my first time eating in a Chinese restaurant. I was mesmerized as I watched Keyoshi's father slurp down a huge bowlful of noodle soup in short order, using only chopsticks while holding the bowl to his lips.

It's strange that, in all that excitement, I still remember our long conversation in the car during the hours-long ride home. A young adult in our congregation was on the verge of leaving for Germany as a "Pax boy" to help rebuild housing destroyed during the war. I was trying to explain to Keyoshi our notion of "serving in the name of Christ." I was surprised by his excitement at hearing of someone sacrificing personally to make a difference in the world.

Then he shared with me some of his own dreams of studying agriculture so that he could someday teach good agriculture to poor people. This Buddhist had a strong service outlook. I remember that car ride as an experience in profound engagement between an idealistic Mennonite and an equally idealistic Buddhist.

On the one hand, I would have still agreed with my church that surely my Mormon and Buddhists friends were going to hell, while we Mennonites would be about the only ones going to heaven. On the other hand, cracks were forming in my certitudes, not least of all because of my crazily curious mind.

When I was a fourteen-year-old doing irrigation duty, heaven and hell occupied my mind. The geography of these places was always clear. Hell was "down there somewhere," and heaven was always "up there somewhere." You have time to ponder when you are irrigating. Water happily gurgled into parched earth, thirstily and noisily lapping it up. I was lying on a ditch bank looking into the sky and pondering the mysteries of my short life. Suddenly a huge problem jumped uninvited into my brain: If the earth is round and China is the other side of the world, then if you were in China, the directions to heaven and hell would be exactly oppo-site to those directions here in Rosemary. So where, then, are heav-en and hell? Are they even physical places?

The other question that tormented me was about Cain, the son of Adam and Eve. According to Genesis, Cain found a wife to marry. How could this be, if his parents were the first parents? If the creation story in Genesis was literally true, how could there be a wife for Cain to start the next generation?

I kept these tormenting thoughts to myself. But they were fis-sures growing in my premodern faith and worldview. One clear question was whether I needed to read the Bible, especially the cre-ation stories, literally. The other was whether God could really love, and save, people who were outsiders and "of the world"—the English. Would the rigid church/world dichotomy held by my church still serve me if I embraced a far-reaching "modern" world-view?

Things were getting messy, chaotic even, in my otherwise well-structured view of the world and the faith.

And Now?

Fifty years later, I keep revisiting the themes of chaos and "the other." My growing up dogmatisms were disoriented. However, I do reaffirm basic certainties arising out of my relationship with a generous God. I happily name myself a Christian, a follower of Jesus, though one who has not answered nearly all the faith ques-tions that continue to arise. And I'm happily a Christian pastor, but that too puts me into almost daily contact with one mess or another.

Pastoring continues to be a messy art, but one I have embraced with love and deep satisfaction. My pastoral vantage point has allowed me sometimes to see the mysterious working of God, whose Spirit is active in people's lives, bringing healing, meaning, whole-ness, and even order out of chaos.

Chapter 2

CALLINGS:

UNEXPECTED INVITATIONS AND SURPRISING HOSPITALITY

Sunday, May 11, 2003, was one of those awesome, tender, sacred days in which it seemed life was filled to overflowing with the grace-filled love of God.

During that morning's worship service it was my privilege to hold and to bless eleven babies. The whole front of the church was filled with parents bringing their infant children forward for a parent-child dedication service. In our tradition we practice believers baptism and invite people to be baptized after they have committed their lives to Jesus. We don't baptize infants, but we give a blessing to infant and parents. We want to communicate that the child is deeply loved by God.

This particular morning radiated warmth, love, blessing, and considerable noise. Infants don't necessarily embrace silence, and the hug of a pastor does not guarantee hushed peace. But to hold eleven babies in my arms, one after the other, whether they were gurgling or crying, and to pray on them the blessing of God and return them to sometimes smiling and sometimes tearful parents, reduced me to quivering. In that ceremony the parents committed themselves to nurturing their child toward God, and the whole congregation committed itself both to support the parents and to participate in raising that child in a loving and accepting community. The church seeks to extend a blessing on infant and parents radiating into the future.

Later that same afternoon, at First Mennonite Church in Kitchener, Ontario, I was able to hug and bless our eldest son as he was ordained to pastoral ministry. Another pastor had blessed him and us when Mark was an infant. I had baptized him in his late teens, and now another had ordained him.

Wave after wave of emotion and tears flowed over me that afternoon, from the beginning of the prelude until the end of the postlude. It caught me by surprise; I hadn't anticipated the flood of feelings. Of course I was pleased with Mark's vocational choice and had strongly affirmed his and the congregation's decision to request ordination. Lydia and I happily joined our larger family circle as we encircled Mark and his family with our love and support.

It's just that I couldn't stop crying. The emotions flowed from many sources, not all of which I understood or could have anticipated. On the one hand, the service brought back memories of my own ordination more than thirty years earlier, in February 1972. At that time, not much was made of ordination, which suited me just fine. Many people in the General Conference Mennonite Church in that era were downplaying the importance of ordination. They were reacting against the inordinate amount of power they thought had been given to some of our clergy. Traditionally Mennonites insisted on "the priesthood of all believers." It seemed quite out of character for pastors to gain so much sacredness and the ordained clergy so much power. When I was growing up, the pulpit had become so holy that only the ordained person could speak from it. Bishops had to receive a second ordination before they were deemed suitably holy to baptize people, serve communion, and officiate at weddings.

But now many wondered why we were setting apart people when our theology was egalitarian? Why were we giving power to one person when the power needed to lie with the people?

So my ordination was a simple and quiet one, almost routine in nature, and somewhat anticlimactic. There was little fanfare leading up to it. There was no interview process to test my theology, competence, or suitability for ministry. It just wasn't a big deal. I recall feeling a certain amount of emotion, but not nearly as much as I experienced with my son's ordination.

Still I don't think the emotions overwhelming me had to do only with memories of my own uneventful and plain ordination or with now participating in Mark's much more celebrative and liturgically colorful one. Instead I felt an overwhelming sense of gratitude, a gut-level thank-you to God for calling me to ministry in the first place, for sustaining me through some forty years of it, and for the churches where I'd lived out this calling. Then to be so deeply aware that God had now also called our son to the same vocation took the controls off my usually in-check guts.

Mark is far more extroverted than I am and more self-confident than I was at his age. He lives easily in the public sphere. In one respect, though, we are both captivated by the same vocational loves. We both love conducting choral music. Mark came close to enrolling in graduate music studies rather than seminary. But here he was being ordained and celebrating his decision to be a pastor.

I too almost chose to become a musician. But the summer before I started seminary, I was invited to come to the Leamington United Mennonite Church in southern Ontario to preach on Sundays and to pastor a huge group of young adults. I was also to form and lead a choir. At the same time I was aware that two Mennonite Bible colleges in Winnipeg were sponsoring a month-long music seminar for Mennonite musicians from across Canada during the month of August. The seminar leaders had invited some big-name choral and vocal musicians from Germany.

I knew I had to attend that seminar, though it didn't make logical sense. My career path was feeling like it was getting set, and the direction was not that of being a musician. I had a fine opportunity to gain some pastoral experience and a bit of funding for it in Leamington. But August belonged to Winnipeg. The Leamington church reluctantly agreed to a shorter term for me.

The month-long music seminar was a taste of heaven to me, a full immersion in my two loves of conducting and singing. I even got to conduct a piece for our final public concert. That month was everything I'd hoped for and dreamt about.

Driving back to Elkhart, Indiana, to begin seminary, I was sated and thrilled. But I knew intuitively that a career in music was not for me. It wasn't logical, but I knew deep within me that God had invited me to be a pastor, not a conductor. I was fully content driving our VW bug in the direction of seminary, and I have been fully content with that decision ever since.

Mark still is very much a musician. He has many opportunities to help make music happen in the community he serves, whether as conductor, pianist, singer, or worship planner.

It seems we indoctrinated him with our musical tastes; there was lots of music by Bach at his ordination. That alone would have been cause for my tears.

This "Calling" Thing

In July 1965 I started my pastoral ministry, and I'm still passionate about it. Pastoring was a totally improbable thing for me to do, and I still marvel at the calling.

Being a pastor was the last thing on my mind as I was growing up in Rosemary, Alberta. I was going to be a farmer; even as a teenager I knew that was clear. At fifteen, as an enthusiastic member of the 4-H club, a prime steer I raised was chosen as the grand champion at the big Eastern Irrigation calf show in Brooks, Alberta. I led the celebration parade through the town that Saturday. My calf was sold for twice as much as the other steers. As excited as I was about this championship, it was sobering to realize that my "pet" might soon be on some neighbors barbecue.

The following year I decided to fatten and groom an Aberdeen Angus steer, a beautiful, pitch-black animal. My champion animal had been an ordinary brown Hereford. I was convinced that the Angus had every bit of the championship caliber the Hereford had. We would again wow the judges. But in one of those inexplicable twists of fate in a teenager's life, the steer wouldn't budge from the truck hauling him to the show. Then he started foaming at the mouth, and just went stark raving mad, probably because of the crowds and the noise.

Suddenly he charged out of the truck and thundered away through the streets of Brooks, with me in hot pursuit. The car horns only intensified his panic—and his speed. I tried to corral him toward the fairgrounds, but by that time we were both exhausted. He had just enough energy left to charge me one final time and pin me to a tree. After I extricated myself from the tree, I borrowed a horse and roped the steer, then dragged him to the stockyards, where they shipped him directly to the butcher shop. I never showed him in the ring, but by this time I was more ready to see him on some neighbor's barbecue.

Still, I had my heart set on being a farmer, but three things intervened. The first was that I wasn't any good at fixing things, and farmers who can't fix things don't last long. My father put it into words one day when I heard him say to neighbors, "That Gary is someday going to become a church worker. He's not good for anything else."

Second, I loved music too much. My plan became to attend Canadian Mennonite Bible College in Winnipeg and study music for a year so I could come back to Rosemary, be a farmer, despite my father's opinion. In Rosemary I would conduct the church choir as my father had for many years. To me, that would be the life—to both farm and make music.

But then, while I was at college, a third thing happened. After being mostly a failure as a high school student, I discovered a love for learning. Somehow one year became four, and though farming was by now receding as my dream, I still wasn't ready to become a pastor. Far from it.

The Blame for Becoming a Pastor

While my father saw so clearly that I wasn't farmer material, my mother thought God might have something special in mind for me. Not that she saw any special piety or gifts in me. No, what she saw mostly was that I was accident-prone. From infancy on I'd lurched from one crisis to another, any one of which could have cost me my life. Mom would just shake her head and say, "Gary, I think God must have something in mind for you. Otherwise I don't know why He keeps sparing your life."

I also blame John Janzen. He was a neighbor and Sunday school teacher for a while when I was an adolescent. One Sunday morning in class, he said totally out of the blue, "You know, someday I think Gary is going to become a preacher just like his grandfather before him." Stunned disbelief was all around. As far as I knew, nobody else in Rosemary saw me that way—and neither did

I. For example, when I joined the church choir at sixteen, a neighbor complained to the deacons about the mischief I had created on his farm that Halloween. And my Sunday school teachers despaired at me always looking for the opposite answers to the ones they wanted. John didn't teach us all that long.

But it was John who'd been involved in my first accident episode. At about a year old, I crawled out to explore the tractor John had just driven into our farmyard and lay down in front of one of the big hind wheels. I guess I thought it was the perfect place for a nap, hidden away like that. John was ready to drive on. Mom had no idea where I'd disappeared to, but for some reason she screamed. She didn't know why; she's not the screaming type. Just as he was releasing the clutch and gunning the motor, John heard the scream and jammed on the brakes. The hind wheel of the tractor made a physical impression on my body, but I crawled away uninjured.

I also blame Menno Wiebe. When I was near the end of studies at Canadian Mennonite Bible College (graduating with both a bachelor's in Christian education and a sacred music diploma), I was married already, and Lydia and I had made careful plans for our future. We had been accepted as students at Bethel College in Newton, Kansas, and would take a year to complete a more fully recognized bachelor's degree. We weren't sure what we'd do after that, though given who my wife was, there were thoughts of something involving the church. Lydia had a very keen mind for thinking theologically, and she had a deep love for the church forged by working through a conflict in her home church. For me, if I was going to be involved in the church, it would probably be in music.

Menno came to us on a Thursday evening, just before I was leaving for camp Assiniboia to lead a weekend workshop on music. He was leading the mission board of the Conference of Mennonites in Canada. After a quick hello, he said to us, "There is a little Mennonite Church near Sudbury, Ontario, Waters Mennonite, which needs an interim pastor for a year. And I think you are just the right couple to go there. I need to know by Monday morning."

No time. No process. No interview. No filling out a Ministerial Leadership Information form. No candidate visit to Sudbury to get acquainted. No vote or invitation from the folk at Waters Menno-nite. Just this totally unexpected invitation from Menno. On Monday morning Lydia and I looked at each other and both said yes at the same time.

Mostly I blame God, of course. I don't think my parents and John and Menno acted on their own. For some strange and crazy reason, God was calling me into ministry despite the improbability of me ever being an adequate pastor. There's a humor-filled grace at work in even imagining those next forty years of ministry, let alone the love and the joy that would fill them.

Waters Mennonite

In early July 1965 Lydia and I were driving through Northern Ontario on our way to Sudbury and Waters Mennonite Church, and I was having panic attacks. In the first place, we had nowhere to live. INCO, a big nickel mining company, was in the boom part of the mining cycle. Workers were flocking to Sudbury and claim-ing every possible house and apartment. For two weeks we found nothing except one small apartment immediately underneath the biggest smoke stack in Copper Cliff, which spewed its smelter poisons in a black, acidy smoke. There was nothing else.

We were in despair until Alvina Martin came to our door. We'd briefly met this small lady wearing the white prayer net on her head at church that first Sunday. Alvina was of Swiss Mennonite back-ground, and they were rather literal about obeying Paul's injunction that women should not pray with head uncovered. I was of Dutch/Russian Mennonite origins, and we had never taken Paul lit-erally on this one. We read the Bible literally on many other things, but not when it came to how women should pray. So I was sur-prised to see this woman wearing a prayer net in church.

Alvina said, "I have been praying that God will give you a place to live." But not only did Alvina pray, she also acted. She knew a rich, elderly widow whose husband had died in the previous year and who was living alone in her mansion (well, to us it looked like a mansion). The house was on an eleven-acre lot overlooking a lake at the foot of the little village of Naughton, about two miles from the church.

Alvina convinced this woman that it was time for her to move into an apartment in Sudbury. And she knew the perfect couple to rent the house: the church's new minister and his wife, but they are very poor and can only afford sixty dollars a month in rent.

So we moved into a Godsend of a house. In the living room stood a gorgeous fireplace, and the house was not only large enough for us to have the whole church over on New Year's Eve, but also fully furnished. Even after the widow took couches and chairs and tables to her new apartment in Sudbury, there was more furniture left behind than we knew what to do with.

One year at the church became two years, but the elderly widow died during our first year in her house. Her estate needed to be settled, so the house sold, and we got our notice to vacate. We'd planned to leave Sudbury on July 2, two weeks after our son, Mark, was born. But the notice stated that we had to leave the house by July 1. God missed it by a day, we joked.

The Swiss Mennonites baptized their young people far younger than we Russian Mennonites did—at eleven or twelve rather than the much more acceptable seventeen or eighteen. They had attracted all kinds of community people to the church, especially Finns, who served their coffee so strong we had to chew on it. Many of these community people weren't so sure yet about this Christian thing, or this Mennonite thing. They tended toward being lapsed Catholic or Lutheran (especially the Finns), maybe Presbyterian or Baptist. A native family just off the reserve came with a whole bunch of kids, the youngest one already over thirteen pounds at birth. One family from the community came with six foster children, a few of whom were emotionally troubled and sometimes troubling. Truth be told, I was a bit afraid of them.

This eclectic bunch simply embraced us. It didn't matter that we were young, foolish, insecure, or inexperienced. It didn't matter that I was way over my head giving advice to a young Catholic couple about birth control, which their own church said was sin. It didn't matter that I was barely out of the teen years myself and could offer very little help to parents struggling with teenagers and their issues. It didn't matter that many of the people on Sunday morning couldn't understand my sermons because I assumed biblical knowledge they didn't have and used clichés they didn't understand.

The congregation just loved us. They overlooked my inexperience and inadequate sermons. Gradually I was able to relax my tight muscles and embrace and love them in return. Maybe that was my biggest lesson as a young pastor: to let the congregation love us and learn to love the people of the congregation. That wasn't automatic and wasn't at all easy. I was too tight inside and didn't know how to let a congregation love me. I was cautious about letting myself get too tangled up in loving a congregation.

It didn't help that two of the deacons of Waters Mennonite Church were far more conservative theologically than I was. They expected things of me I couldn't deliver, and they expected language in preaching and actions in the community that weren't mine. I had to have it out with them and name our differences. Despite those differences, they loved us, and I learned to love them. I still marvel at my deep fondness for that church even forty years later.

My First Sermon

On July 18, 1965, I preached for the first time at Waters Mennonite Church. I chose my texts from Matthew 10:37, "Whoever loves father or mother more than me is not worthy of me; and whoever loves son or daughter more than me is not worthy of me"; and Matthew 16:24-26, "Then Jesus told his disciples, 'If any want to become my followers, let them deny themselves and take up their cross and follow me. For those who want to save their life will lose it, and those who lose their life for my sake will find it. For what will it profit them if they gain the whole world but forfeit their life? Or what will they give in return for their life?'"

These texts may seem inappropriate to inflict on a new congregation, but I was probably projecting an inner struggle with abandoning my mother, a recent widow, to move across the country. It felt something like choosing to love God more than her, and I was having a difficult time with that.

My father had died about a year earlier from complications following a heart attack. Mom had spent a year on the farm mourning him and then sold the farm with plans to move west to the

Fraser Valley in British Columbia and start a new life and career as a nurse's aide. I was heading the opposite direction, east to northern Ontario. I wouldn't be around to help dispose of the farm and help her with a relocation that was wrenching in its physical and emotional complexity. I felt guilty about that, and I was still grieving the loss of my dad and my home.

At the other end of the country, I was far away from the family drama clutching my heart. Following God's illusive call into pastoral ministry felt like taking up a huge cross and losing my life.

While there's a deep truth in these texts, in the end following Jesus doesn't at all feel like abandoning parents or losing one's life. I may have preached about "finding security in an insecure world," which was the sermon's title, but it is still profoundly true that you save your life by trying to follow God's will, while you may lose it trying to follow only your own desires.

After forty years, what I realize is that the move to Waters Mennonite was not self-denial or losing my life, but finding a life that is richer, deeper, and more filled with love and amazement at God's work than I could ever have imagined. Grace and love have far overshadowed my incompetence and my often-weak faith. God has continued to work through my human foibles, often despite my best or worst efforts.

There were struggles of faith and crisis of calling still awaiting me after Waters Mennonite, but God had put me on a journey. And I'm still enjoying the ride.

In the end what sustains my passion for ministry is the people who invite me into their lives. It is such a sacred thing to be welcomed into the deep recesses of someone's life and soul. Over and over I am privileged to enter someone's life for a short moment to listen to their story, to share with them, or cry or laugh with them, perhaps to challenge them, and sometimes to pray with them. In all of this there are always deeper questions to ask: Where is God active in your life and experience? Where can you look for the holy presence in this part of your story? Often I see transformation occurring—in their life and in mine. But even when despair and pain need to run their course, there may already be signs of healing.

Recently I read again that first sermon at Waters Mennonite—

and cringed a lot. I think now that I probably preached about security because I was so afraid and insecure myself. At the time, Lydia and I still hadn't found a place to live, and the transition of the previous few months had totally overwhelmed me. I was insecure in faith, calling, marriage, and myself. I could only cling to the promise that God would somehow see us through.

I was also insecure in reading and interpreting the Bible (still am, for that matter). My college days were a time when I read the Bible with new eyes and a new mindset. I hadn't heard about categories like modern and premodern back then, but the two were beginning to clash in a big way. I was already skeptical about the literal Bible interpretation of my youth. Even then, the reading of Genesis that dated the creation of the world some six thousand years ago seemed more and more implausible.

A Bell Saleswoman Comes Calling

I'm surprised by the number of people who want to connect with God but are either alienated from the church or just don't want to bother with it. They frequently invite me into their lives, not because of who I am but because to them I represent the "office" of ministry.

I rarely use the title "reverend." To the congregation, I'm simply Gary. While some conversations abruptly end when people find out I'm a clergyman, others are surprisingly open.

Once I was relaxing at home in the evening and happened to be wearing a T-shirt that had been a fiftieth birthday gift from one of my children. It stated boldly, "I'm not 50. I'm 18 with 32 years of experience." There was a knock, and I opened the door to a woman in her early twenties. She took one look at me and burst out laughing. Nonplussed, it took me a while to figure out that it was the T-shirt, not my face, that she found so hilarious.

"Hey, Sonya," she yelled to her partner knocking on our neighbor's door. "You gotta come see this." Our neighbors weren't answering their door, so Sonya came right over. "This is really cool. I love the T-shirt. Isn't it something?"

"Awesome, Veronica," Sonya said.

I finally asked them who they were and what they wanted.

Turns out they were working for Bell Telephone and were concerned about us not getting in on the special Bell was offering: twenty-five percent off all long-distance calls. But they needed some information first.

"Age?"

"58."

"Employer?"

"Toronto United Mennonite Church."

"You mean, you're, like, a priest?" asked Sonya, a bit awed.

"Close. I'm a minister. A Mennonite minister."

"Mennonite? Which book do you study?"

"Which book?" I asked perplexed.

"Yeah, which book? Well, like the Book of Mormon. Are you a Mormon?"

"No, I'm a Mennonite, not a Mormon. We read the Bible, like all other Christians."

"You're a minister, a real minister?" Veronica asked. "Would you pray for me? Please? Would you pray for me? I don't care which church you are. I need someone to pray for me."

"Of course, I'll be glad to pray for you. Is there something specific you want to pray about?"

"I'm pretty messed up right now," said the laughing one as she started to cry. "Right now I've just broken up a very important relationship. But that's because I'm so messed up. I need to get back to church. I want to get back to church. I've left God out of my life the last while, and I think that's why everything is falling apart. I really need you to pray for me. Will you? Here is my name on this card. Veronica." So I prayed for Veronica—and for Sonya—and smiled at the strange providence of God.

In this short encounter between total strangers were hilarious laughter, tears of pain, and a deep sense of need. It didn't matter one bit that I was Mennonite. I could have been Catholic, Pentecostal, or Mormon. What was important was that as a clergyman I represented faith to them.

I didn't possess a particularly hospitable spirit when I opened the door that evening. I'm inclined to give salespeople short shrift, but how could I resist such laughter?

Hospitality is central to my understanding of the gospel because that is what I saw in my parents. Mom and Dad were not particularly articulate about their faith, and we didn't talk much about faith at home. Dad was introverted (like I am), though he could be a sparkling conversationalist. They lived a winsome, attractive faith, and they were both active in and committed to the church.

With genuinely hospitable hearts, they nurtured healthy relationships, including with all their neighbors, some of whom were difficult characters. One of dad's idiosyncrasies was that he co-owned pieces of farm machinery with various neighbors. While this made economic sense, I believe there were other motives. Such relationships committed the neighbors to working out tensions when there were competing self-interests, like when each thought his wheat field was ready to harvest, but they all shared the same combine. As far as I know, co-owning farm machinery with various neighbors never created an irresolvable conflict.

My parents opened their home and their lives to all kinds of people. They were open to new ideas, including new theological ideas. They encouraged and supported and blessed their four sons in their educational and vocational pursuits, which took us away from the home community and some times far from the comfortable parameters of their own world. My mother, at age ninety-four, still lives out this hospitable and relational spirit, showering love and acceptance on grandchildren especially, even when they make faith and ethical choices far different than her own.

It wasn't so much words and beliefs; it was a lived-out faith. This was what won me to my own faith.

He Eats with Sinners

Lived-out faith often got Jesus into trouble. He didn't accept the limits to hospitality that his people had encoded into law and practice. It was terribly unsettling for them to see Jesus comfortably entering the lives of people who were so obviously unrespectable. The accusation was true: "He welcomes sinners and eats with them" (Luke 15:2).

One of the realities of life is that there are insiders and outsiders in every human group. We either belong or don't belong. Many people spend their entire lives trying to move from not belonging to belonging in a school, family, friendship circle, youth group, or church. We do our best to enter the "in" group at work or to fit in on the playground, in the peer circle, on the team, in the gang.

Some people have a way of being at the center of things, knowing they belong, perhaps even feeling the heavy burden of responsibility for the group. They feel close to those inside, know all the rules and expectations of belonging, and stay easily within the comfort zone. Others know themselves to be on the periphery of a circle, on the outside looking in, mostly excluded and often feeling bad about it. Sometimes, feeling hurt and lonely, they act out in bizarre ways in efforts to crash into the center of things.

Sometimes the barriers to the inner circle lie within the outsider: lack of confidence to squeeze in, a chip on the shoulder that puts others off, choosing values other than those of the group, being critical of everything that happens. These attitudes may mask deep pain that can't be easily healed, such as a lack of self-esteem or a history of rejections.

Often though, the barriers are within the insiders. In attitudes or words they say, "Keep away. Don't come too close. You are different from us. You have a different skin color. You aren't one of us ethnically. We aren't sure about your lifestyle. You worship and think differently than we do. What if your children would fall in love with our children and want to marry them?"

Every identifiable group struggles with insiders and outsiders, including most families and churches. In every church are those who know and feel themselves to be at the center of things. They often have been there for a long time. They hold power and make decisions. They do important things, and they belong.

Every church also has those who feel themselves to be on the outside looking in. They feel marginal, not fully accepted, and they don't have much power. When they speak, no one seems to notice or listen. They aren't often invited into the homes and lives of the in-crowd. Some have experienced deep pain with the church. Some aren't sure if they know the unspoken expectations of the insiders. They hesitate because something feels strange or uncomfortable, unfamiliar, or unwelcoming. Or they have been labeled as sinners.

Guess Who's Coming to Dinner

With his parables, Jesus runs roughshod over the clear lines between insiders and outsiders and sometimes reverses the roles. Certainly he blurs the lines; at times he shocks everybody by naming traditional insiders as outsiders in the kingdom of God and naming the seemingly sinful people as genuine insiders.

Luke 14 starts as criticism of those who clearly saw themselves on the inside of religious and political life. A Pharisee has invited Jesus to a banquet at his house on the Sabbath day. On the surface the invitation is a friendly gesture of hospitality, except that the Pharisee has invited others who were important and powerful and clearly an inner circle. There will be some interesting dynamics unleashed. All will watch Jesus closely because they know he stands outside their usual power politicking.

The guests take their places at the banquet table, with careful attention to social position and claims to honor. It is normal in their circles to jockey for position by trying to get nearest the place of highest honor. Jesus stands back and observes the unfolding scene, then makes comment in which he warns guests at a banquet not to seek the places of honor, lest they be asked to move for a more distinguished guest.

"Choose the lowest place," he is advising, "and perhaps the host will invite you to a place of higher honor."

The parable is finished, but Jesus isn't. He seeks out his host, the one who invited him, and confronts him with the challenge to invite outsiders to his next banquet instead of the usual insiders he welcomes for political reasons. Jesus challenges the whole structure of social climbing, seeking honor, and laying claim to insider privilege and position.

Then he tells them a pointed parable: Someone planned a great banquet. The guest list included many big shots of religious, political, and social life. But these insiders already go to many banquets and are probably expected to return the favor. They will have to try to throw a yet more smashing party. Even though banquets have by now become a bit blasé and boring, they accept the invitation. You never really like to say no to someone directly.

While they're talking with a fake smile to the one giving the invitation, they're thinking that this one won't really score them enough brownie points to make it worthwhile. They've heard all the nice, proper speeches and sermons so many times and have in fact given them many times themselves. They have "insider fatigue." Even as they say yes to the invitation, they're planning their excuses:

> "I bought some land and really have to attend to it. I am really excited about seeing it. Please accept my very sincere regrets."
>
> "I bought some oxen and need to spend some time training them and familiarizing them with their new surroundings. I'm sure you understand my huge disappointment in not being able to come."
>
> "I just got married. Wonderful woman. I'm sure you can appreciate my wanting to spend more time with her on our honeymoon. Please invite me again."

Underneath the surface of these excuses lies a deeper awareness. They don't trust the one extending the invitation to keep it an insiders-only affair. They know that the host invites people from the other side of the tracks and has a history of bringing unsavory characters into his home for these banquets. They don't want to be contaminated with these outsiders.

The host becomes angry. Enough of playing these political games! "Go and invite the outsiders," he says to his servants. "Invite those who will be excited about coming, those on the margins—the poor, the alienated, the ones with little social prestige, the ones who don't know etiquette, the ones who haven't had the courage to enter the worship space of the temple, the ones you thought were unclean, impure, almost certainly sinners. Invite the Gentiles. Invite them all. I want my house full for a great party."

His servants have already anticipated this request. They've already done all that. They know how their master operates. He has a reputation. No wonder the rejections came thick and fast from the insiders.

Yet there is shock and outrage. We insiders are scandalized that the host (God) is inviting people from outside our safe religious and social structures. We hadn't expected to see the face of God in any but insider faces. We hadn't expected God's invitation to feast with dirty people. We hadn't expected God's party to be so much fun in the first place, and now we'd missed it. Since when did religious parties stop being tame, run-of-the-mill, be-there-just-to-be-seen affairs? When did they become so lively and so much fun?

The unexpectedly invited outsiders too are shocked. They hadn't expected to crack the inner circle. They had long rationalized that the insider parties were dull and not affairs they'd want to be at anyway. But once there, the food is great and the dancing goes on all night. They feel exhilarated. And accepted. All their pent-up spiritual longings come bursting to the surface and are satisfied.

Maybe when we insiders give up control of the guest list, we too will discover that it's a terrific banquet. God is doing the inviting with a guest list that shocks us. When God is the host, we all are guests. Everyone is having a wonderful time, and there's laughter enough to infect even the most incorrigible sourpusses and the most straight-laced pastors. God's party pulses with life and surprises. The lines are blurred between insiders and outsiders. The dancing is going on all night.

It's all made possible when we stop trying to keep out the people God is inviting.

An Angel Wearing a Hijab

As a pastor, I am an insider in the Mennonite church. Not so in some other contexts.

In 2000, we took a six-month sabbatical and lived in Cairo on a Mennonite Central Committee assignment. While there, MCC asked us to spend two weeks in Iran as a part of an interfaith exchange program. We came to Iran excited but apprehensive, wanting to dialogue with Muslims and look through positive eyes at an Islamic world painted so negatively by the West.

The two weeks were full of memorable encounters, trips, formal visits, and fascinating sightseeing. One blistering-hot day, we were visiting Kashan, a city on the edge of the central desert. In the morning we'd been to the village of Qamsar, halfway up the mountains on the outskirts of Kashan, to see the production of the famed "rose petal water" and to visit a small orchard. The orchard was like an overgrown jungle, a proliferation of various kinds of fruit trees that defied systems and neat rows. Nothing had been pruned or thinned or sprayed. Our hosts spread a Persian carpet under the trees and offered us a fine meal of kebabs, complete with rose petal water and some very delicious fruit. Then we all napped on that carpet.

There we were, Christians and Muslims relaxing together on a carpet in the middle of this profusion of nature, experiencing each other as fellow human beings enjoying life but also needing sleep. On one corner was Lydia, a Christian woman, covered head to toe in the required black. On another corner I snoozed. The Muslim cleric who was our weeklong guide had hung up his overcoat and turban on a branch; he snored lightly on yet another corner. On the fourth lay our Turkish Muslim chauffeur. We were all at ease as we rested together.

The wildness of the orchard and the improbability of that scene on the carpet serves as a metaphor to me. Sometimes when we stop cultivating for a while and stop using rules to keep us apart, when we hang our religious barriers on a branch for a time, a God-given moment can happen. Our simple human connections are priceless.

However, one day at the end of our stay in Iran, we needed an angel to help us. Early the next morning we were to fly back to Cairo. That evening we asked each other about any unfulfilled dreams for our trip. Lydia was disappointed that we hadn't been in more Iranian homes and that she had not been able to talk in-depth with more Iranian women. She'd have that opportunity, but in a way we never would have expected.

Everything proceeded normally at the airport early the next morning. We cleared customs easily, as we hadn't bought any Persian carpets. The baggage was checked and we had our boarding passes in hand. Only one more line—passport control.

"You can't get on the plane," said an officer-in-training. She was no doubt looking at visas more carefully than others might. "Your visa is not valid."

Cold sweat.

"But what is wrong with it? Don't we have a valid two-week visa?"

"Your visa date is okay, but your visa limits you to a seven-day stay within those dates. See right here. Seven days within the fourteen-day period. And you have been here twelve days already. Therefore, your visa is no longer valid. You must cancel your flight and go to the department of alien affairs to extend your visa."

No amount of discussing with higher officials helped. We retrieved our luggage and tried to make flight reservations for the next day, but the airline refused. They didn't expect us to have our visa renewal by then. In some turmoil we took a taxi to alien affairs, where nobody spoke English. We were on the edge of panic when an angel appeared.

"Do you need any help? I speak Farsi and English." Victoria had come to alien affairs to get visa extensions for her two children. Altogether ours would be a six-and-a-half hour process, which itself was a miracle. In that time we procured about twenty signatures, visited two different banks to pay money and obtain receipts, had our pictures taken, appeared in court before a judge, and paid a fine.

As we were about to go before the judge, Victoria quickly took some socks from her purse and put them on. A woman can't face a judge in Iran with bare feet. Alas, Lydia wasn't wearing any socks. We had expected to be out of Iran early in the morning, so she had gone barefoot in her sandals under her hijab. Now she desperately needed socks and persuaded me to let her wear mine. I faced the judge sock-less.

We were now lawbreakers in Iran, convicted of overstaying our visa. We paid a fine of about one American dollar each. Victoria, though, stayed with us the entire morning and into the afternoon. Had she not, I'm sure the process would have lasted some days rather than some hours. She canceled her appointments for the day to see us through. She interpreted for us and calmly pled our case. Amazingly we received our visa extension just minutes before the office closed for the day.

Our next frustration was that the plane for the next morning was already booked full, but we managed to get the last two seats for the following morning.

Victoria wasn't finished with her angelic work. When we finally left alien affairs with our visas in hand, she invited us home for dinner that evening. Her American husband had died several years earlier of cancer, and she wanted to live in Iran. It was more financially feasible—her American widows pension would go further here—and because she wanted her five- and seven-year-old children to grow up with Iranian culture. We had a wonderful evening with her and her children, and gradually the panic and stress of the day abated and we relaxed into the enjoyment of new friendship.

Lydia got her wish to be invited into another Iranian home and have an in-depth conversation with an Iranian Muslim woman. It seemed God took Lydia's wishes for a prayer.

Hospitality Reflects God's Heart

I believe that hospitality is at the center of the gospel. Jesus shows us the hospitality at the heart of God for all humans. By his life and teaching, Jesus invites us to open our lives to others, including strangers and enemies. At its best, the church lives out this calling to open its doors to the outsider. But the church, like all human communities, will sometimes close its doors in fear or in a false sense of righteousness. While God continues to use the church, flawed and inadequate as it is, God will not be limited by the church. God's work is bigger than any one church or denomination or religion can contain.

Occasionally I see a glimpse of that bigger work. In the meanwhile I'm content to be a pastor of a small, struggling, faithful, wonderful, amazing, gifted, failure-prone group of God's people who sometimes manage to live out the hospitality of God.

In June 2006, our second son, Kendall, and Charleen, his wife of just over a year, began a summer assignment as co-pastors of Harrow Mennonite Church in the southeastern corner of Ontario. They had just finished their first year of master's of divinity studies at Associated Mennonite Biblical Seminary in Indiana. Both Kendall and Charleen have resisted a bit God's invitation to them to become pastors, I think.

In 1969, Kendall came late into this world. His doctor predicted an early birth, so we waited a full month for his arrival. But that gave us some extra time to plan my one and only experience of being a pioneer. When Mark was born I'd slept through the intense labor and delivery on a hospital guest cot far enough away from the action to be oblivious to it. Not this time, we determined.

"I'm planning on being in on the delivery," I announced boldly to our doctor in Goshen, Indiana. But this had never been done before in that hospital. Back then, doctors worried that the father, watching his wife give painful birth, would need medical attention himself. Besides, it just wasn't proper.

But we insisted. Reluctantly our doctor agreed—if the right nurses were on call at that moment. They were, and so I attended Kendall's arrival, and suddenly I was handed a wrinkled, overdue, squalling baby. The medical people all left the room, leaving mother, father, and son to their own intimacies and bonding. We held Kendall in a big embrace; we prayed and cried our thanks and our joy, and the memory and the emotion became engraved forever within us.

This son is very unlike his older brother, even though the two are close. He takes more after his father than his mother, especially in being on the introverted side when it comes to engaging with people. From birth he had a mind of his own, never particularly caring about peer pressure or the fads that drove others his age or the pressures of his large extended family.

There seemed to be too many pastors already in the families of both his parents for him to move in that direction himself. Grandparents, uncles and aunts, cousins, a parent, and finally a brother were all pastors. Not Kendall. He studied some theology and music at Canadian Mennonite Bible College. He too loves conducting and singing. Then he completed a master's in medieval studies in Toronto. Maybe history was for him.

Off he went to Cairo for three years as a volunteer with Mennonite Central Committee, teaching English as a second language to students at a Coptic Orthodox cathedral and seminary there. It was in Cairo that our relationship with him took a turn.

I had a six-month sabbatical leave in 2000, which Lydia and

I spent in Cairo, also with MCC. She was teaching theology at the evangelical seminary there. I was resting, reflecting, journaling, and trying to be a pastoral presence in the MCC unit. By then Kendall knew Cairo and the culture and quite a bit of Arabic, and he confidently oriented his parents to life in Egypt, brazenly navigating the chaos of Cairo traffic.

We were really quite dependent on him, which changed something important in our relationship. It's often hard for parents to give full independence to their children and to relate with them in a fully mutual way. But in Cairo, Kendall was the experienced one. His contacts and friendships got us into a number of Egyptian homes. And that loosed us from any vestiges of unhealthy parental control.

In Cairo Kendall would occasionally preach and lead worship at St. Andrews Church with its Lutheran liturgy. The people of that church recognized his gifts and his spirit, all independently of his pastor-centered family.

When he returned to Toronto, our church saw the same gifts in him and invited him to be on the preaching team. And at thirty-five he fell in love, which delighted us to no end. He was absolutely smitten with Charleen, as we were.

We actually knew Charleen before Kendall did. She and another woman lived in our house while we were in Egypt. All we really knew about her was that she was Dutch Reformed and she had made some acquaintance with Mennonites through a stint of Mennonite Voluntary Service in Minneapolis-St. Paul.

Kendall and Charleen met at Toronto United Mennonite Church. She was working for the Yonge Street Mission as a kind of chaplain to children and families. He was teaching English as a second language in our New Life Center. Both of them were looking for new challenges and opportunities, which led them to seminary after they got married. Neither of them really expected that. Or at best they thought that seminary might be in the distant "someday" future. But both were soon thriving on seminary life and studies and moving toward God's invitation to pastoral ministry.

As they arrived in Harrow for their summer pastoral assignment, I was thrilled, delighted, and afraid. I still am a parent who worries sometimes when I needn't. I pray that the Harrow Church, and the others to follow, will be as inviting and hospitable to them as the churches enduring my pastoral ministry have been to us.

Chapter 3

BLESSINGS:

PREACHING LIKE A JACKASS, WITH HELP FROM A PROPHET

In July of 1965 Lydia and I were driving through Northern Ontario in our Volkswagen Bug, getting closer and closer to Sudbury, Ontario. In a total upheaval of plans, we'd been persuaded a few months earlier (by the Holy Spirit?), to temporarily abort our plans for further education while I took a one-year interim pastorate at Waters Mennonite Church. As a recent graduate of Canadian Mennonite Bible College (CMBC) and a new husband, I was becoming more and more aware that I was totally unprepared for what might lie ahead.

Lydia and I met at "bridal college," as CMBC was sometimes jokingly called then. We faced each other across a Ping-Pong table in my first week at the college, though I hardly noticed her during the game. But a week later my new friend John and I thought we wanted to go on a Friday evening date. Neither of us had any particular girl in mind to ask out; we hardly knew any girls there. So we got out the student list. When I traced down to the name Neufeld, Lydia, I vaguely remembered the Ping-Pong game. Not a bad player, I remembered, for a girl!

I needed courage because I had little of it when it came to asking girls out. I had almost no experience at it. Growing up with three brothers and no sisters made me afraid of girls. Make that terrified.

But I was at college, and it was time to take terror in hand and call someone quickly before all courage evaporated. Neufeld, Lydia. No, she didn't remember a Gary. Good thing. So she said yes. Marie, the girl whom John had called, also said yes. Good start.

My beloved Calgary Stampeders of the Canadian Football League were in town to play the hated Winnipeg Blue-Bombers. I hadn't been to a football game for three years, and I was excited about the game and about having a date. Lydia had absolutely no interest in football. I can't imagine why she even agreed to go, and she soon regretted it. I was so into the game that I forgot to talk to her.

John and Marie on the other hand were chatting away, almost oblivious to the game. "They at least talked together," Lydia groused to me later. "I was really envious of Marie." It was not a good start to a dating relationship.

We didn't date the next few years. I wanted to, but Lydia didn't. But I was falling in love with her. Clearly she didn't reciprocate my feelings and had no interest in dating someone who didn't know how to talk and was totally absorbed in football.

There was much in Lydia to fall in love with. She was so full of life, energy, and fun. There was also such a depth to her, a deep spiritual core, faith, and a sense of personhood. She was serious about life and the issues with which we students struggled. She was obviously intelligent, which scared me a bit, because I had been such a mediocre student through high school. I also thought, and still think, her very, very beautiful.

By the end of our second year at CMBC we did study some Greek together. She assumed she was tutoring me, and I gladly let myself be tutored. It did gnaw at me a bit that we could study the same things for the same length of time and yet she got better grades.

I suppose I wore her out with my persistence, because she said yes to another date. This time we went to an opera, Mozart's *Così fan tutte*. In the summer after our third year, we got married.

Lydia always loved theological and biblical studies. She probably would have been a pastor had she been a man, but that was not possible for a woman in the Mennonite Church back then. Despite her brilliant mind, outstanding grades, and insights about the church, she received no encouragement to continue theological studies.

Lydia always loved discussing and debating. That all started in the peach orchard on the farm where her dad and her two brothers (and sometimes two sisters) and she had rousing discussions while picking peaches. I can imagine the ladders themselves swaying in the breeze of their verbiage. Animated and vocal with strong opinions easily and loudly shared, they vigorously explored everything from theology to dating.

What amazed me when I entered this family was how thoroughly they all enjoyed this almost combative give-and-take. Lydia and her father especially had a relationship that included strongly expressed opinions and convictions, sometimes even flashes of anger, but never any that threatened their deep and fond relationship with each other. My own family was much less expressive, though also close. Lydia and I struggled to cope with these differences. But it has been an incredible gift to me to learn from my spouse to be comfortable with rigorous and vigorous expressions of opinions, whether of agreement or of disagreement.

When Lydia was in her mid-forties, after our three children were adolescents and less dependent on a stay-at-home mom, Lydia resumed her theological studies. She had considered upgrading her teaching credentials and going back to teach elementary school. But her teaching certificate from Ontario was not accepted in Alberta, so instead of repeating three years of undergraduate studies, she enrolled in a master's of theology program at Newman Theological College, a Catholic graduate school in Edmonton. Just when Lydia was dreaming of doing a doctorate in theology, and Toronto School of Theology seemed to be almost the only place in Canada to do it, the Toronto United Mennonite Church invited me to be their pastor. This convergence of opportunities brought us to Toronto in the fall of 1987.

Learning How Much We Need Women in the Choir

The two of us have always debated theology and biblical interpretations, Lydia perhaps a bit more strongly than I. This has immeasurably shaped my preaching and teaching. Animated discussions of things theological and constructive critiques of each other's work has been a significant part of our relationship.

Through my theologian wife I caught up with theological trends, partly through her insistence that I read feminist theology and attend a conference called "Women Doing Theology," which she had helped establish.

I was apprehensive at that conference in May 2001, one of only a few men amid two hundred women in the great hall of Conrad Grebel College in Waterloo. It was perhaps not surprising that few men applied, even though the brochure stated that both men and women were invited. Throughout most of Christian history, men have done theology while women listened from the outside. It seemed fair to me to have men listen in, so I went. Lydia was one of the main presenters.

She has commented often about how it feels to be the only woman at a male-dominated meeting, which is what church has mostly been for women until quite recently. "I won't ever again be the only token woman at one of those meetings," she has said more than once.

I can be reasonably comfortable in various settings, including some in which I am in the minority. So I sailed into the conference in good spirits, looking forward to some good theological stimulation—until we got to the first hymn as we started our worship. I belted out my bass line loudly and with confidence. But amid the beautiful all-female choir with only soprano and alto sounds, my bass voice seemed like an intrusion. I hesitantly ventured a quarter-volume bass line. Even so, a few eyes turn my way. Were they eyes of welcome or of reproach? I was unsettled where I had not expected to be.

The women's choir has become a metaphor for me. Over centuries—probably since the early decades after the death of Jesus—theology has been a male choir thing with only one or two women's voices daring to squeak out a line before being silenced. A male-voiced Gregorian chant is beautiful all on its own, I suppose, just as a women's choir can be beautiful. But over the long run, it becomes boring if that's all you hear. And a male choir is limiting, less than God intended, and keeps women on the outside.

Only a few men among two hundred women? Why should we come to hear women doing theology? I suppose we men forget that all thoughts about and experiences of God are filtered through our humanness, which includes being male or female. Men and women just might have different insights into the nature of God. Throughout most of Christian history, theology has been filtered mostly through male lenses—and prejudices—and voiced primarily by men. Surely it is time to allow women's voices to enter the conversation. But even now, it seems to me, male theologians, including Mennonite theologians, are still not taking these women's voices seriously enough.

I thoroughly enjoy singing in our Toronto United Mennonite male quartet. Those male voices and harmonies resonate within me. The other three in the quartet are superb singers; two of them sing professionally in opera and oratorio. But in the church and in theology I want to sing in a mixed choir and hear all voices, male and female.

I long for the time when the church will invite women's voices as a full part of the theological choir. Till then I will gladly feel exposed and discombobulated in the occasional women's theological choir.

In the meantime, Lydia and I teach a course entitled Theology of Church and Ministry to master's-level students at Conrad Grebel University College. Earlier in our marriage, doing so would have been disastrous. Our personalities, teaching style, and approaches were so different that we would have frustrated each other too much. But we have each mellowed some, or at least we understand each other better. Mostly we see these differences as complementary. Teaching together now is one of the satisfying experiences of our partnership. But back in 1965, we still had many things to sort out in our relationship, and I had many things to sort out about being a pastor.

In the little town of Wawa in Northern Ontario, my panic boiled over. We were on our way to Sudbury and the Waters Mennonite Church, where I was to be pastor. I had been quiet and brooding for several hours. For me the silence wasn't unusual. While I was quiet on the outside, there was turmoil on the inside. Suddenly, in the middle of the town of Wawa, I burst out, "Lydia,

I think I know what the theme of my first sermon is going to be. But what am I going to preach on after that?"

I asked myself that question for the next forty years, but I never ran out of topics or themes or texts or ideas. While there has always been more than enough to preach about, I still panic when nothing seems clear. Tuesday is the critical day, when I begin sermon preparation and realize that I have no idea where to start. But then I remember that the pool of possibilities is always bigger than I have time to use, and the leftover crumbs fill many baskets.

In Bible college, two worldviews clashed. Some of our professors were of the old school, explaining *Biblische Geschichte* (Bible stories) simply, without reference to context, and in German. Most younger professors had drunk more deeply at the well of modernist critical studies and challenged us with an entirely new way of reading the Scriptures, especially those from the Old Testament. They lit my imagination just as they shook my foundations and helped me claim a faith that could no longer be contained in the old wine skins.

But integrating new ways of approaching faith and Scripture takes longer than a few years, and my interpretive insecurity continued. While my lifelong fascination with Scripture continues, I have to confess that I probably would not study with the same rigor if I were not forced, sermon by sermon, to do so. Often the texts unsettle me in some way if I read them carefully enough, and I don't preclude new understandings by being locked into a favored interpretation.

A Jackass's Tale

Some Old Testament stories, for example, eventually went in totally new directions for me. In the middle of the book of Numbers, we find a speaking donkey. This tale must have delighted the Hebrews; I can imagine them telling and retelling it, probably with some wonderful embellishments.

I wonder if the listeners of the story stumbled over the idea that a donkey can speak, a question that troubles modern readers. I doubt the Hebrews worried about it. In the first place, if God wants a donkey to speak, who were they to object, especially when it was the Moabites who were forced to listen. But the Hebrews didn't need to interpret this story literally. It was simply a wonderful tale of God using a donkey to foil the evil scheming of a terrified king. It might remind us to lighten up our own readings of the Scriptures and see a tale like this as a humorous parable. There is, after all, a rich playfulness in our Scriptures that surprises and sometimes exasperates us. Truth slips through our defenses while we're chuckling.

In the story, the Moabite king Balak was facing a flood of Israelite refugees and feared they would one day be powerful enemies because they were a particularly prolific people. As Balak said, "A people has come out of Egypt; they have spread over the face of the earth, and they have settled next to me" (Numbers 22:5). So he plotted and schemed to find ways to drive the foreigners out. In a panic Balak immediately considered siccing his army on the refugees, but his forces were small and pitiable compared to the hordes of Hebrews.

His terror grew, and he tried to hire the prophet Balaam to cast a curse on the Israelites. "There must be standard fees for curses," Balak thought, and he sent officials with bags of gold to entice Balaam to Moab.

But a strange thing happened when Balaam prayed. Israel's God, Yahweh, answered him and discouraged him from issuing the curse. So Balaam sent his regrets to Balak, who was dismayed but sent a more powerful delegation with yet more gold and promises of huge honors. Who could blame Balaam for finally agreeing? For such wealth and prestige he would be ready to curse anyone.

But Balaam was not the villain in the story. Though not a Hebrew, he seemed open to listening to Yahweh, and he talked about "the command of the Lord my God." But he was finally blinded by the glitter of gold. As he rode off, rehearsing his curse and counting his shekels, an angel of a very ticked off Yahweh blocked the road with sword in hand. Balaam couldn't see the angel, but the donkey could. Ah, the humor of God. The prophet—the "see-er"— couldn't see the angel, but his ass could.

The donkey veered off into the field. "Stupid donkey. Here's a whack for your stupidity." Next the angel stood at a narrow point between two vineyards. To avoid decapitation, the donkey scraped against a wall, hurting Balaam's foot. Now Balaam was getting very ticked off. "Here's another whack. Can't you see where you're going?" A third time the angel stood, sword in hand, at the narrowest place in the road, leaving no escape route. So the donkey lay down.

Furious, Balaam beat the donkey mercilessly, and suddenly it gained the power of speech. "I would like to explain who the real jackass in the situation is," it said. "You're the one who can't see the angel ready to cut you down. I'm only trying to protect you." At that, Balaam's eyes were finally opened and he saw the angel. The angel told a kneeling Balaam to proceed but to "speak only what I tell you to speak" (22:35). Balaam meets King Balak and told him, "How can I curse whom God has not cursed? How can I denounce those whom the Lord has not denounced?" (23:8).

All of us, pastors included, seem convinced that God is on our side and will ever curse those we curse. But how can we curse what God has blessed, and how can we bless what God has cursed? If only we could see which is which. But, like Balaam, we are often blind, and then we learn that some stupid ass sees what we can't.

Am I totally missing the point by applying this humor-filled story to serious life issues now? Bear with me. In this particular tale God is ready to bless a bunch of worn-out, down-on-their-luck but still rebellious Hebrews just passing through Moab. Maybe God just likes blessing. If only we could see whom God wants to bless—refugees, poor people, discouraged people, and the homeless—and not stand in the way, not try to add our curse to the many already hurled at those we've traditionally considered worthless, such as the aboriginal peoples of North America. Our governments, aided and abetted by our churches, have had a centuries-long record of cursing First Nations people, of trying to destroy their culture and self-worth, of abusing their children in our residential schools, of trying to assimilate them into mainstream culture. All along God was trying to bless them, but we couldn't see that until the flaming sword of their pathos-filled stories broke through our blindness. Or until their lawsuits forced us to pay attention.

Our Own Culpability

Lydia and I inadvertently and naively became a part of a less-than-blessed government policy when we adopted our daughter. We had two boys by then and wanted a girl. We were open to adopting a First Nations child unaware that adopting these children into families like ours was part of a government policy to assimilate aboriginals into white society. We were approved for the adoption; then we waited.

On Friday of Thanksgiving weekend 1973 Lydia startled me by saying, "Today they're going to call. I feel intuitively that today we are going to hear about our baby." There had been no word from anybody for six months, and I was skeptical. All day Lydia waited for the phone to ring. At 4:30, disappointment etched her face. "I guess I was wrong," she said. "The office is closed by now." But at 4:55 the call came that a native girl, aged two and a half, was ready for us to adopt.

Our daughter, Kristen, joined our family circle, and our lives were changed and blessed. She was a delightful and beautiful girl, though sometimes a stress on our equilibrium. One of her favorite games was hide-and-seek, but she played a variation—"hide and scare the daylights out of your parents." She'd hide in the hall closet and when an unsuspecting parent opened the door, she'd scream "Boo!" and we'd gray prematurely. Much to my delight, I've heard that our granddaughter is playing the same game on her mother.

Several Christmases ago Kristen invited her biological mother to spend Christmas with us. At the age of nineteen Kristen began a search for her biological and cultural roots. Her original adoption documents had her parents' names blacked out, but by holding it to light, we made out a last name. The Alberta telephone directory attached that name to a family network from the Siksika Indian Reserve near Gleichen. A friend of ours had contacts there and passed the word around that Kristen was looking for her biological family. Within several weeks she received a telephone call from a half-sister. The search took her to within fifty miles of where I grew up.

For Kristen, finding the family was a mixed blessing and brought both healing and pain. The healing came through making connections with her biological family, her culture, and her identity as a native person. The pain was in becoming aware of chronic alcoholism in the family, especially of her mother, Heather. She had been forced into one of the infamous residential schools, through which the Canadian government tried to root out native identity and force assimilation into white society. Many residential school alumni later turned to alcohol to quench the resulting despair and emptiness.

Heather found the courage to live the last years of her life sober. Mother and daughter established a relationship, and Kristen's mother spent Christmas 2003 with us in Toronto. Kristen sat her three parents down together on our couch and gave us each a matching gift, candle holders, that symbolized the uniting of her two families. The powerful moment seemed suspended in sacredness and felt like the completing of a circle. Later that spring Kristen was able to be with Heather when she died and to help plan the funeral.

When we adopted Kristen, Lydia and I were naive about native issues and about how to raise an adopted aboriginal daughter. When Kristen was about 8 years old we took her to the Edmonton Museum, where we spent time in front of the native exhibit, with its big tepee. I wanted to take her picture in it, but it meant nothing to her and, in fact, embarrassed her. We hadn't helped her understand her identity or history, so the gesture was meaningless to her.

As Kristen grew up, we gradually learned more about native culture, issues, anger, and spirituality. Because we hadn't been wise enough as parents to introduce her into this world, she more or less had to do it on her own and then bring us along. This process included both anger and pain as well as new awareness.

As a youngster, I had visited the Siksika Reserve with a school hockey team that played a team of young natives. Our prejudices then were strong. We saw natives as lazy, and they'd want to fight at the drop of the puck. But now my background and Kristen's have been brought together by adoption. My eyes have been opened to the curses heaped on natives by white society. Through our daughter we have been privileged to enter another cultural and spiritual story.

Now we have three wonderful, beautiful, black-haired, dark-skinned grandchildren living close by. They tease me when I listen to my classical music. "That is just Opa's powwow music," they say. I muse over the deep insights that pour spontaneously out of their mouths. I swell with pride when I witness the oldest, who has become a fine native dancer, in full native regalia.

Once eight-year-old Mitchell asked, after we had said grace before a meal, "Oma, Opa, why do you pray?"

"Why do you think we pray"? asked Oma.

He pondered a moment, then said, "Because you are white?"

We told him that, in his house they don't say grace before meals, but his mother prays, just differently. She too gives thanks to the Creator, the Great Spirit, and participates in spiritual rituals like powwows and burning sweet grass. But our grandson soon tired of this overextended God talk and continued eating his meatloaf.

The next day his mother called us, laughing. "Mom, Dad, what are you teaching my son?"

"What do you mean, what are we teaching your son?"

"Do you know what he asked me today? 'When did God and the Great Spirit become friends?'"

Someone told us once, "You sure brought some much needed color into your family life." Curses have been turned to blessings in all our lives. Understanding has replaced prejudices. Through Kristen we have begun to stand in solidarity with First Nations people as they insist on being treated with dignity. We have been sensitized to hear new voices in a chorus singing for justice, and we delight in the spontaneous laughter and joy that this daughter brings into our family circle.

Do We Curse or Bless?

We humans, Christians included, do not have a good record of discerning who is blessed or cursed by God. "Surely," we think, "our enemies are worthy of God's curse." If only it were so simple. For centuries we thought it okay to curse slaves, especially if they were a different color. For centuries the church cursed women as being inferior, more prone to sin than men, and incapable of any real leadership in society or in the church.

More recently we've cursed people on social assistance. (Ontario still "claws-back" child support money from the federal government to welfare recipients, that is, they reduce social assistance claim by the amount of the federal government's child benefit, which every family with children can claim. Apparently only people well off are supposed to enjoy this federal largess). We are inclined to lay curses on the Islamic world, convinced that all Muslims are terrorists. We routinely inflict curses on people of nonheterosexual orientation, not to mention the curses that conservatives and liberals throw at each other.

I wonder what angel with flaming sword in hand is trying to stop us from completely destroying our environment with the curse of our consumptive consumerism. How many cancer-related deaths will it take before we hear the donkey speak? How many days gasping for breath in our polluted air? How many cycles of drought and flood will we tolerate before our eyes open to the reality ahead? Or will we blindly accept our destruction of God's good earth?

I suppose the church is like Balaam, not always knowing whom to bless and sometimes ending up cursing the wrong people. I hope that sometimes the church can be the jackass seeing things others can't, ready to absorb the anger of a Balaam in order to prevent his decapitation.

Does God really speak through talking donkeys? For that matter, does God really speak through braying preachers?

The Preaching Team

At my ordination in 1972 I received Reinhold Niebuhr's *Leaves from the Notebook of a Tamed Cynic* (Meridian Books, World Publishing, 1970) as a gift. A good friend from college, Rodney Sawatsky, thought I needed the reflective wisdom of this man writing about his first years in ministry in Detroit. In a piece that caught my imagination Niebuhr writes,

> Now that I have preached about a dozen sermons I find that I am repeating myself. A different text simply means a different pretext for saying the same thing over again. . . .
>
> I almost dread the approach of a new Sabbath. I don't

know whether I can ever accustom myself to the task of bringing light and inspiration in regular weekly installments. . . . How in the world can you reconcile the inevitability of Sunday and its tasks with the moods and caprices of the soul? The prophet speaks only when he is inspired. The parish preacher must speak whether he is inspired or not. I wonder whether it is possible to live on a high enough plane to do that without sinning against the Holy Spirit. (pp. 22-23)

I have felt very strongly that as pastor, I should not do all the preaching in our church. On the one hand, I don't think I have enough spiritual resources to do so. I don't think I could preach week after week without sinning against the Holy Spirit, as Niebuhr suggests, and without impoverishing the congregation. Any church is the poorer for it when the people hear the same preacher all the time. God does not speak through only one voice, one interpretation of Scripture. A church needs to hear the voices of its laypeople.

The Mennonite tradition of having four or five ordained lay preachers had much merit. These men (at that time, only men) were chosen from the congregation and continued earning a living in their chosen professions, but they were expected to take turns preaching. Most didn't have the opportunity for biblical or theological education. Some of them could take only a few courses at a Bible school. But they studied Scripture diligently, and each had a unique voice. They weren't always skilled communicators or exegetes; growing up I remember being impatient with some homiletic offerings. But they provided a balance to the ministry of one preacher, however skilled.

Another part of my theological heritage I value highly is the notion of the "hermeneutic community," which is a fancy way of recognizing that no one has a monopoly on interpreting the Bible. As long as they are open to being guided by the Holy Spirit, anyone can share insights and wisdom and inspiration about a text that will benefit the whole community. All believers are expected to read the Bible together and help interpret it within their context.

The political and religious authorities in the medieval world were appalled by this notion and thought it highly dangerous. But the sixteenth-century Reformation took the control of the Bible and its interpretation out of the hands of the hierarchy and gave it to ordinary Christians. That was dangerous then and is still dangerous today. Sometimes the local church will understand a text or an issue differently than its larger denomination does. This creates tension but also new windows to see what God is doing.

When I was ordained, it was important to me to preserve some of the richness of this lay ministry heritage. In my candidacy negotiations with First Mennonite Church in Edmonton in the fall of 1971, where I was pastor for almost sixteen years, and then with Toronto United Mennonite Church, where I was pastor until 2007, I said that I would be very happy to preach two Sundays per month, but no more. The other Sundays needed to be filled with lay preachers from within the congregation or with occasional guest preachers, and I would try to encourage and train lay preachers. Both churches agreed to this.

I was thrilled when I came to Toronto to learn that a preaching team was already in place. Four laypeople had been chosen by a congregational discernment process and served for two-year terms. They joined with me to take responsibility for preaching and for nurturing the spiritual life of the congregation. Together we discerned the direction of the preaching and what issues needed to be addressed. We reflected together on the context in which we were living and the kind of gospel word needed for that context.

The preaching team continues to try to "grow preachers." Every meeting begins with an opening reflection by a team member, which usually leads to a spirited discussion about the perils and joys of preaching. Then we spend time providing feedback to anyone who has preached since the last meeting. We challenge each other to find our true preaching voice.

Our congregation like every congregation is rich in people who bring enormous gifts to preaching. Together they represent a broad base of experience in Christian living and reflection on the Bible. I absolutely delight in the dynamic, life-giving ministry of our preaching team.

A Sinister Biblical Hero

When we became aware of the number of women connected to our congregation who had been abused, often sexually, the preaching team felt that the congregation needed to become sensitive to issues of sexual abuse and family trauma. They decided that during preaching times the congregation would be made aware of the deep pain that some people carried, though personal stories would not be shared. For a pertinent Scripture passage, the team zeroed in on the story of David and Bathsheba. So I read the stories of David and tried to ponder the experience of Bathsheba through new eyes.

Bathsheba was enjoying the warm, late-afternoon sun, taking a bath on the roof of her house. There she was, naked, beautiful, and in the eyes of at least one beholder, very sensuous. David saw her that way and was filled with lust for her.

"Who is she?" he demanded. "Bring her to me!" David is king and has complete power over her. And he rapes her (see 2 Samuel 11).

The heading on my NRSV translation of the Bible reads, "David Commits Adultery with Bathsheba." I question this title. This was not adultery. Adultery is when two people with equal power decide mutually to be unfaithful to their own spouses and have sex with each other. That would be sin enough. But this was surely not adultery. It was rape. Bathsheba has no choice. Whatever happened to good King David?

Some interpreters blame Bathsheba, not David, for this sexual encounter. She was bathing naked in full view of the king. She must have been trying to entice him. What was he to do? My argument is that King David holds all the power. He sent messengers to get her, and she would have had little choice. The king has to be fully responsible for their sexual encounter. Later, he does confess his guilt.

David's story unfolds like a vintage success story, almost a fairy tale. He had been the youngest and most inconsequential of eight sons of Jesse, a shepherd. Young David was minding his own business and his sheep one day when the prophet Samuel visited the homestead with his anointing oil, looking for the next king of Israel. Jesse's oldest sons filed by, each impressive in his own way, but none of them got God's signal. Finally, the text says, David came. "Now he was ruddy [with red hair or vigorous health], and had beautiful eyes, and was handsome" (1 Samuel 16:12). I'm not sure why those are qualities for kingship, but "the Lord said, 'Rise and anoint him; for this is the one.' Then Samuel took the horn of oil, and anointed him in the presence of his brothers; and the Spirit of the Lord came mightily upon David from that day forward" (verses 12-13).

In most of the stories from the books of Kings and Samuel, a very favorable portrait of David is drawn. He is a hero. As a young lad he played his harp for King Saul and soothed him enough to relieve him of his afflictions (see 1 Samuel 16). While still a boy soldier, David had the courage to face the giant Goliath when more seasoned warriors didn't. Though he wasn't strong enough to wear a soldier's armor, David met Goliath armed only with a sling and five stones, and killed him (see 1 Samuel 17).

There are also the wonderful stories of David's friendship with Saul's son Jonathan. Then David married Saul's daughter Michal. Theirs seemed to have been a genuinely loving relationship and marriage (see 1 Samuel 18, 20).

Eventually King Saul felt threatened by David's growing power and popularity and tried to kill him. There are many stories of David's daring escapes, but when he finally had Saul cornered, David graciously spared the king's life (see 1 Samuel 24, 26).

David did become king and was a very good one. He ruled wisely and united the kingdom with Jerusalem as its capital. The prophet Nathan had words of praise for this good king (see 2 Samuel 7:3-17).

David married a few more wives, as kings are wont to do. There was Abigail (1 Samuel 25:39) and then Ahinoam (25:43). There are more stories of successful wars and of particular kindnesses. Then suddenly we are confronted by the story of Bathsheba.

The Coverup

Bathsheba becomes pregnant from this rape, and the king wants to hush it up. He brings Bathsheba's husband, Uriah, back from the battlefront, where he is one of David's best generals. "Surely," David thinks, "he will sleep with his wife. Then how is he to know that the baby isn't his?" But Uriah is a man of character and strength. He will not enjoy the comforts of home and the joy of sex while his soldiers are in depravation and perhaps even dying in battle.

Plan B. David tries to get Uriah drunk. Perhaps then he will sleep with his wife. Even that doesn't work. Finally David orders the commander of the army to take Uriah back into battle, put him where the fighting is fiercest, and then abandon him there. The scheme works, and Uriah is killed. David has murdered him.

Problem solved. Now he can legitimately take the new widow as his wife. Everything is covered over and handled beautifully. The secret is kept hidden. Bathsheba is now David's wife.

What about Bathsheba? Almost nothing is said of her in the Scriptures. The whole story is told from David's point of view. We are told nothing about Bathsheba's feelings, point of view, personality, or pain. She is simply the wife of Uriah the Hittite, a warrior.

The child conceived in the rape is born sickly and dies. The account suggests that the child's death is punishment for David's sin (see 2 Samuel 12). I don't know how to deal with that; I don't believe that God actively makes a child suffer for the sins of the father, though surely many children suffer for their fathers' sins. Scriptures do tell how David's surviving children were scarred and dysfunctional. David's son Ammon rapes his sister Tamar (see 2 Samuel 13). His son Absalom revolts against his father (see 2 Samuel 15-18).

Bathsheba's whole life is shaken and changed forever. All the old values and familiarities have been destroyed. She has to live with her rapist and the murderer of her husband. Her grief and pain find no expression in the record.

At the end of David's story, Bathsheba again enters briefly. David is on his deathbed. Two of his sons are fighting for succession. Adonijah, David's son with Haggith, another of his wives, announces that he is king. But Bathsheba pleads with David to make Solomon, the son born to her and David, king instead (see 1 Kings 1). Bathsheba has a hand in making Solomon the next king of Israel, but for the most part she remains a very minor footnote in the story.

But getting back to David, he's just breathed a sigh of relief. He will get away with it all after all—until a prophet shows up, the same one who earlier praised and anointed him. Nathan comes to visit the king and innocently begins to tell him a story about a rich man and a poor man. The rich man has many sheep. The poor man only one: a family pet that was "like a daughter to him" (2 Samuel 12:3). The rich man, needing a lamb to host a guest, slaughters the poor man's pet for the banquet. Outraged at the injustice, David can hardly listen to the end of the story. He is ready to go after the rich man and kill him.

In effect, Nathan says to David, "You are that man! You, David, king of Israel, are the rich man. You have it all. The Lord has given you everything. But what do you do? You steal Uriah's wife from him, you rape her, then you have Uriah killed. You did this evil thing and then tried to cover it up in deception. But the Lord sees it."

So now the whole nation knows. And what does King David do? He repents. He confesses. He says, "I have done evil" (2 Samuel 12:13). This confession is surprising on several counts. First, it's surprising that a simple story about a lamb broke through a king's defenses and layers of self-deception. Second, a prophet with only spiritual authority dared to confront a king. And finally, and most shocking, the story was recorded for the whole world to read.

King David's confession and repentance do not heal the wounds of his victims. The text is mostly silent on the pain Bathsheba carried. This raises for me questions about the male-centered nature of the Bible's point of view. Why did David get all the space in the story and Bathsheba almost none? Can this story be read and told in today's egalitarian world?

Can such an androcentric story give us any measure of hope in the context of sexual abuse? Yes, it can, because it shows how the most powerful abusers can be held to account. By some miracle, they may even confess. I find it inspiring to read a story of a prophet who had the courage to confront the abuser in such a way that the abuser couldn't miss the point. Can the church be such a prophet?

Prophets Within the Interpretive Circle

At the root of the ongoing struggles in our denomination around human sexuality and the issue of membership and leadership roles for homosexuals is the question of who should be included in the interpretive circle. Should traditional interpretations have the final say, regardless of new biblical insights? Or should conference statements or the *Confession of Faith*? Can a local church do its own interpretive work on the biblical texts and discern the will of God for itself? What if this discernment is not in line with that of the denomination?

Giving the Bible to the people is still dangerous; some lay people could become prophets.

Toronto United Mennonite Church (TUMC), the last church I pastored and of which I am still a member, has tried to include itself in the hermeneutic process struggling with issues of human sexuality. It is one of the most "conference-minded" congregations I know, always discerning with the denomination's wisdom before it. In the end, our own interpretive work moved us to somewhat more open stances toward those who are homosexual than that of the larger denomination. Others from our denomination have challenged not only our interpretation (a challenge we welcome), but also our right to interpret in the first place, a challenge that seems to negate the Anabaptist notion of hermeneutic community.

The reality is that within our congregation we also have divergent and conflicting interpretations of Scripture, causing considerable internal conflict around this issue. But we're learning to bring our voice and conviction to the table in modest decibels, and we're trying to listen to other voices and interpretations. At our best we discern together under the guidance of the Holy Spirit, and at our worst we hurt each other in the process.

Sometimes the questions come in great intensity. Does God still speak to our context from a book several thousand years old? Can God speak through fallible interpreters of those stories? What happens when interpretations diverge as much as they do today? Are they instruments for God's voice today?

The hermeneutic community isn't a panacea either. Wouldn't it just be easier to have the scholars or the denominational headquarters tell us the meaning of a text and the right solution to especially contentious issues? Sometimes the preaching team offers more challenges and critiques than I'm ready to live with. But I continue to delight in studying the Scriptures. I usually enjoyed this preaching thing, but it is one of the pastoral tasks I miss deeply now that I'm retired. I value our preaching team and have deep convictions about the need for every local congregation to play an important role in the larger hermeneutical task of the Christian church.

During my seminary days in the late sixties and early seventies, preaching was definitely "out." It was an age of anti-everything, and the "establishment" was bad, church included. If you wanted to actually help people, it was best to become a social worker, not a pastor. Social workers were relevant; pastors weren't. Preaching was definitely not where it was at. It was the worst form of communication imaginable.

I know that seers can't always see, and I know that a donkey can sometimes speak more truth than I can. I hope then that I can laugh with a God who will find a way to speak today, whether through a donkey, a prophet, or even a preacher. God will use any and all of these to stop our world from cursing those whom God wants to bless and to spread God's blessing around, even to those who experience mostly curses.

Chapter 4

BOUNDARIES:
TENDING THE GARDEN AND DEALING WITH WEEDS

The garden on the farm in Rosemary was huge. It had to supply our vegetable needs for a whole year, as well as cucumbers and raspberries for relatives from Didsbury, Alberta. The garden had three sides. To the south was a large irrigation ditch that brought life-giving water from the canal, which took its water from the Bow River's Bassano Dam. Just beyond the ditch was a gravel road leading into town. To the west, fronting our driveway and our farmyard, rose a row of fast-growing poplar trees, which were a nuisance. They died young and shed their sappy fuzz indiscriminately in spring. To the north Dad planted a row of willow trees, a clear border between our garden and the wheat field.

The garden's various kinds of vegetables and fruits needed clear parameters to separate them. But there were no lines marking ends of rows; they could simply grow longer to the east if needed. There was room to expand, which was a scary thought to a young boy with hoe in hand. Because we irrigated the garden, both vegetables and weeds grew fast and large, which meant lots of hoeing and weeding.

On hot summer days when I was dying to go swimming with my friends, my mother demanded, "First hoe three rows of corn, then you can go." I hated hoeing, especially when it was sizzling hot. The nearby water hole was an almost unbearable temptation when muscles ached, blisters formed on my hands, and my mouth was parched with thirst. For me, weeds spoiled our almost perfect garden.

But one neighbor boy seemed to like pulling weeds. His family had come from Germany in the early 1950s. Roughly my age, about thirteen, he hired himself out to another neighbor for twenty-five cents a day to pull weeds from a wheat field. All day he cruised through a sixty-acre field, pulling out the yellow mustard weeds and thistles. When he was done, there wasn't a speck of yellow in that waving sea of green. But to me, twenty-five cents a day wasn't enough for that much hard work.

Weeding at Church?

I thought the evaluation was fair: "Gary, as a pastor you are good at welcoming people into church membership. But you are not good at taking people off the membership rolls. Sometimes the church needs to discipline people, and sometimes you need to clean out the names of those who aren't really a part of us anymore." I pleaded guilty, but with extenuating circumstances.

One of the realities of urban church life is high mobility. People come and go all the time. They move to Toronto to do graduate work, then leave for a job in New York or cities beyond. Or they tire of frenetic urban life and leave for an acreage near a small town.

Last Sunday three families told us they're leaving our church— one for a five-year Mennonite Central Committee assignment in Africa, one to do graduate work in the United States, and one to find more peace and quiet in a smaller Ontario community. While I celebrate the new opportunities for each of them, I mourn the loss because I have been both pastor and friend to those moving away.

This mobility thing is really difficult. People are drawn into the congregation. They begin to offer their unique gifts of self and leadership; they form deep relationships; and then they're gone. The whole church feels the loss.

These old relationships can't be replaced, but to survive as a church we have to be good at welcoming new people into membership. Is it really worth the effort and risk of forming new relationships if these members eventually leave?

In our church we have a rather long process for joining the congregation. If people come from another Christian tradition, we ask them to take a three-month "faith exploration" course to become familiar with the Mennonite Church. We then ask them to invite a present church member to become a "faith partner" who will mentor and encourage them. We even invite them to share their story with the whole congregation. Then we ask them to publicly answer some questions, the main one being, "Are you willing, this day, to renew your desire to follow Jesus Christ and allow Him to become Lord in all of your life?"

We don't ask them to leave behind any gifts or heritage from their previous denomination. They don't need to agree with us on every point of doctrine. We don't expect them to name Menno Simons as one of their new heroes of faith. We want to hear mainly about their commitment to Jesus Christ.

When they answer yes, we welcome them into membership and make our own commitment to them: "We commit ourselves to watch over you and one another with a heart of concern and caring. We pledge our willingness to offer and to receive forgiveness in the redeemed community. We joyfully accept you as partners."

The care, support, and accountability we pledge is a form of discipling each other in our attempt to follow Jesus. When we say that following Jesus is central to who we are, we take membership in our Christian community seriously. Being hospitable to newcomers is part of the invitational nature of the gospel. To share our understanding of who Jesus is, we respond to people in need, listen to their pain, and invite outsiders to become insiders.

Many of us find this difficult. We don't easily open our hearts to new people. Our impulse is to guard the church and its core values, identity, and beliefs. At its worst, this impulse is to protect our political power, to be judgmental of other people's sins, and to cling to the fantasy that only we know what it means to follow Jesus.

Every community struggles with these impulses. But if the church doesn't keep inviting people in, it risks spiritual death.

One danger we fear in opening our spiritual home is that we will change when new people enter. We will need to take on more people's pain, and we won't be fully in control of our group identity anymore. Maybe some of our convictions will be challenged, and the church will feel less manageable, neat, and tidy. New people may not appreciate our favorite hymns or resonate with our particular style of worship. It can be difficult to navigate the bridge between insiders and outsiders.

For me, the issues are these: How do you keep a garden, that is, the church, contained within appropriate parameters but open enough to grow? And how do you keep weeds out of a garden in an ever-changing ecosystem, that is, how does a church stay centered in its identity and vision amid a changing culture?

One of our worship leaders brings new spiritual energy when she periodically leads our worship. Her heritage is black Southern Baptist, which means hallelujahs thrown around and lively old gospel hymns with a lot of clapping. Not traditional Mennonite style. Some folks love it, but a few are less enthusiastic.

One woman from Uganda is a wonderful African drummer. While some of us like the energy this brings to some songs, not everyone cares for African drums in church. Come to think of it, not everyone appreciates the music of Bach either.

Once, at a wedding in our church, the couple asked a soloist to sing Charles Gounod's "Ave Maria," traditionally heard at Catholic weddings. The couple had Catholic backgrounds in South and Central America. Can we Mennonites abide an adoration of the virgin Mary in a wedding service?

Discipline in Church

Welcoming new members adds some complexity to community life. What about when insiders start moving the other way and look like they're becoming outsiders again? What does a community do about those losing their commitment to the church?

People leave the church for many different reasons. They may be hurt, disillusioned, or angry; they may feel they can't express their pain or despair; they may be losing their faith or losing interest in worship. Someone may be in some sinful mess, like having an affair, and feel it is just better to disappear. What does the church do then?

I am not good at following rules in dealing with those kinds of messes. Nor do I like weeding out names of people who have left the church for various reasons but want to keep their names on the rolls. I can easily write a letter suggesting that "since you have been away from Toronto a number of years already, I invite you to consider transferring your church membership to a church in your community." But I don't easily write a letter saying, "We hereby release you from your membership at TUMC." My skin isn't thick enough for such agony.

It seemed easy for Menno Simons. We Mennonites are named after him. My faith heritage includes the practice of "banning." Menno banned people who fell into sin or who "erred" theologically. A banned person was to be shunned. Even a spouse was expected to keep a banned partner out of the marriage bed.

The purpose of banning was not punishment; rather it was to win the banned person back to faith and back to fellowship by pointing out that person's sins or errors. It sounds merciful when compared to the method most Christians exercised during the Reformation—burning at the stake!

But banning is not practiced anymore among most Mennonite groups. We no longer follow Menno in this. Part of the reason may be that our tolerant culture predisposes us to think that what people do is their own business. But I hope the reason is deeper than that. I hope it has to do with being more pastoral and less public in trying to keep people accountable to their commitments. The pastoral way, as banning was intended to be, is to invite people back to faith and community. The invitation needs to be non-threatening and redemptive, never punitive.

Joe

Joe gave the impression of having a giant chip on his shoulder. He didn't raise his voice much, but he routinely offered us a "critique" that was often spot on. He saw things that we didn't and that needed to be pointed out. We needed his voice among us. What we didn't need was his anger.

I'm inclined to confront people by inviting them to be aware of the gentle, loving, forgiving God active in their lives. So I had an issue with Joe's angry tone of voice, but usually not with his critiques. We braced ourselves and crossed our arms in front of us in defense when he hurled his considerable insights at us. As our summer student minister once responded to him, "When you swing a two by four at us, we are going to duck."

Joe never officially joined our church, though he participated fully with us for a number of years. But it was always from the edge. Though we may have seen him as an insider, I think he saw himself as always an outsider who was never fully heard. He railed against some of the "very foolish and even unfaithful" decisions he thought the church made, and then he stopped coming.

Superficially his departure was a relief; angry gadflies are not easy to live with. On a deeper level, his leaving was a great loss. No one can replace his sharp, penetrating insights, his analytical mind, his lack of fear in naming our corporate sins. I pondered our inability to address his deeper angers and to draw him fully into membership, and our helplessness in the face of his leaving.

Jill

Jill came crying into my office. She was a Baptist, she said, and didn't really know who the Mennonites were, but she felt she couldn't go to her pastor because she had committed too serious a sin. She was convinced she couldn't go to her parents because they would kick her out of their home. So she wanted to speak with someone she didn't know.

Jill was pregnant and unmarried. It had happened in the heat of a passionate moment with her boyfriend. "We only made love once, though," she explained. "We want to get married this Friday evening. Will you marry us?" She assumed that marriage would make everything right and cancel out her sin, as it were. But she was too afraid to go to her parents or her pastor.

I wasn't ready to marry them that Friday evening. I wasn't ready to marry them without a lot of processing. I did meet with the couple. Eventually Jill confided in her parents, and they didn't kick her out of the house, although they were upset. They went with Jill and her boyfriend to meet with their pastor, who, though also upset, agreed to help them process their situation. Later he officiated their wedding. I rejoiced with them in the healing of those relationships and in the good beginnings to their marriage.

Karin

Karin burst into my office without knocking or saying hello. I had never seen her before. "Why do Mennonites hate Catholics so much?" she demanded to know. Then she burst out crying. How do I say hello to a yelling, crying woman I have never laid eyes on, who didn't even knock before accosting me?

Her painful story had to do with a boyfriend—a Mennonite boyfriend. Their relationship was moving toward talk about marriage. He gathered his courage and invited her to meet his parents. He didn't think they would approve his marrying a Catholic, and he was right. They wouldn't even invite her into the house, and they made her stand outside while they told her they wouldn't let their Mennonite son marry a Catholic.

Now her question—Why do Mennonites hate Catholics so much?—made sense.

"My priest won't marry us," she continued. "He won't marry a Catholic and a Mennonite. Will you marry us?"

"I will gladly meet with the two of you," I said, "and the question of whether I will officiate your wedding will become clear to all of us."

We met a number of times and I discovered a beautiful, deep faith in Karin and in her Mennonite fiancé. They were married in our church. The couple invited his parents to the wedding, but they refused to attend and bless the marriage with their presence. The couple was crushed, and I was very angry with the parents. This couple created a strong, healthy, faith-filled family, but his parents didn't even acknowledge the grandchildren born to them.

I assume that the pain runs deep in both the parents who disowned their son and in the young couple cut adrift. I imagine that the parents needed to develop a thick layer of calluses over their emotions so that they could cope with putting principle over relationship. Or did daily pain still creep through their anger? For the young couple, I think that the pain of rejection must have felt like a daily wounding.

What Do We Do with Weeds?

Paul took us for a walk through his eleven-acre natural habitat near Sherwood Park, Alberta. He is a biologist and environ-mentalist. Though he's almost six and a half feet tall, he doesn't look imposing because he's on the lanky side and hunches over a bit. He looks fully at home in the woods or in a canoe.

Paul has strong opinions about the stupid things we do to our environment and to the church. My friendship with him has grown through many years of sharing deeply on family and church matters. Our children have spent time in each other's homes. Paul and I have even done some book writing together; I contributed to his book *God-Man-Land: Interrelationship Programs for Camps* (Faith and Life Press, 1978).

Paul has a defined garden plot on those eleven acres, where nature is mostly free to run its natural course. His garden isn't nearly as clean as I like to keep mine. "Weeds," he snorts. "No such thing as weeds. All they are is native species that thrive on native soil, often more useful than the stuff we try to replace them with. There is no such thing as weeds. Let them grow."

I knew a sermon was coming.

"People want neatness and order in their lives and in their gardens and in the church," Paul continued. "But nature thrives on chaos. Nature thrives on diversity and chaos. Humans want only order and monoculture. How boring can you get? And look what we do in the church? We want a pure church where we kick out sinners or at least people with different sins than our own. We try to nail everything down in creeds and confessions and elimi-nate all weeds. It doesn't work. There's no interesting life then. Why can't we learn from nature?"

Like his many observations about our environment, Paul's ser-mons are always short, pithy, and pungent, whether delivered on his acreage or occasionally in church. Maybe that's why my chil-dren always preferred Paul's sermons to mine.

We humans are uncomfortable with an unrestrained prolifera-tion of nature running amok. The problem is that we can be more productive with monoculture. Naturally a farmer is going to plant a big field of one kind of crop, say oats. Or a fish farm on the Pacific Ocean is going to grow only one kind of fish, say Coho salmon. A forestry company is going to want to clear-cut a mountain forest and replant the area with one kind of replacement tree. A church planter is going to target one class of people or ethnic group to build a new church with. It is more productive that way, and far more efficient.

But the mono method is also much more vulnerable to disease. Fish farms have many disease problems because of lack of diversity. Much of our crop farming is bedeviled by similar problems because we plant huge patches of land with only one plant. Biodiversity doesn't require nearly as much pesticide and herbicide, and it provides better protection against disease.

My brother Don, a close friend of Paul, is a plant pathologist. He went to college to become a better farmer but didn't seem to know when to quit his studies. He never did make it back to the farm. He had too much fun in high school almost blowing up the science lab and generally paying more attention to those things that intrigued him about the evolutionary process than in digging irrigation ditches or throwing hay bails.

In college he became fascinated with crop diseases, not farming methods. He specialized after a while in rust diseases in oats and wheat. His lab at the University of Manitoba would help plant breeders develop new rust-resistance varieties. Rust, like all diseases, is adaptable, and the job of keeping ahead of its relentless encroachment is never-ending. So Don has published prodigious numbers of research papers and traveled the world delivering lectures.

Probably an easier way to deal with rust would be not to plant such big fields of one kind of grain. An easier solution would be a more chaotic mix of crops, using much smaller fields and increasing biodiversity. But you can't farm efficiently that way. Today's big machines couldn't even turn around in a small field. So we need pathologists to breed in resistance and chemists to help us burn out weeds.

Monoculture in the church opens us to rampant theological disease, whether to violence-prone fundamentalism or anemic liberalism. An ecosystem flourishes best with a chaotic proliferation of species. But as an ecosystem matures, the biggest and strongest species eventually take control and eliminate smaller, weaker ones. A mature system will then become rather stagnant.

Nature has its own way of bringing new life again. A forest fire, for example, will radically alter the entire system and allow for diverse new life to flourish again.

Multiculturalism in nature and in society is complex. A natural ecosystem, even when it starts out with a profusion of species, allows the strongest to triumph and eventually stagnates. An occasional fire is needed. Is this necessary in the church too?

A Parable About Weeds

Last spring Lydia was really ticked off with me. She had planted some sweet peas around the telephone pole on our front lawn. They would create some beauty later in summer. But she forgot to tell me, so I took them for weeds and pulled them out.

In the parable of the weeds among the wheat, Jesus cautions us that harvesting is God's work. When we try to pull out the weeds we tend to uproot the wheat as well. Jesus said,

> "The kingdom of heaven may be compared to someone who sowed good seed in his field; but while everybody was asleep, an enemy came and sowed weeds among the wheat, and then went away. So when the plants came up and bore grain, then the weeds appeared as well. And the slaves of the householder came and said to him, 'Master, did you not sow good seed in your field? Where, then, did these weeds come from?' He answered, 'An enemy has done this.' The slaves said to him, 'Then do you want us to go and gather them?' But he replied, 'No; for in gathering the weeds you would uproot the wheat along with them. Let both of them grow together until the harvest; and at harvest time I will tell the reapers, Collect the weeds first and bind them in bundles to be burned, but gather the wheat into my barn." (Matthew 13:24-30)

A lifetime of conditioning makes me reach for the hoe when I spot a weed in my garden, so this parable sits uneasily in my farmer's heart.

There is rich irony here. During the Reformation, the Reformers challenged the Anabaptists with this parable. The Anabaptists were critical of the church for having so much dead wood, so many people who claimed they believed in Jesus but whose lives gave little evidence of it. They argued that infant baptism created a church in which everybody was "in" without genuine Christian faith. The church the Anabaptists wanted to create, based on the New Testament, practiced adult believers baptism. Only those who made an adult commitment to Christ were baptized.

The Reformers countered with the parable of the wheat and the weeds, noting that Jesus said to let the weeds be and not pull them out. In other words, just accept the Christendom model of a church in which everyone is "in" by virtue of their baptism as infants, regardless of whether or not there is any real faith visible in them.

The irony is that as a theological heir of these Anabaptists, I'm not quite as ready to pull out the weeds as they were. But the whole church looks different today. Christendom is disappearing, and in our secularized society, most people who do go to church now claim the personal faith on which the Anabaptists insisted. People no longer tend to go to church just to be seen there.

So maybe my friend Paul has understood this parable after all. Let the weeds grow. Put away your hoe—at least in church, if not in your vegetable garden.

Accepting Other Plants

One of the things that attracted me to Toronto United Mennonite Church in 1987 when I was a candidate for pastor was the variety of faces in the congregation. I also heard a variety of opinions. There were rigorous theological debates and arguments about issues like the practical implications of peace theology: should it translate into a rejection of capital punishment? There were already a number of people in the church who didn't have a Mennonite background: should communion be reserved for only adult, baptized believers, as was our tradition?

Today this complexity has increased dramatically. We could not have imagined the variety of people of different racial and faith backgrounds. Our differences in education, vocation, income levels, theology, gifts, and needs are vast. We can't reach consensus on the hot issues of our day. We bring different assumptions to the interpretation of Scripture.

I continue to be excited by the rich blessing and ferment this creates. But it's also an immense challenge. How does a group find unity when there's so much difference? What is the common core, the center, the glue that holds it all together? What happens when deeply held faith convictions are poles apart? Can we hold and express these convictions without demanding that others conform to them? Can we learn to trust each other when we profoundly disagree? Will we be able to disagree in love? Or do we have to pull out the weeds?

I'm always fascinated by some of the "wild" vegetables and flowers that manage to grow in my cultivated plots. Somehow there are always some tomato seeds out of a compost heap or acorns a squirrel has buried among the flowers. After having survived a freezing winter, the seeds take root and grow where they're not supposed to. I often leave the little seedlings be, mostly out of curiosity but also out of respect for their hardiness.

This spring several tulips showed up right where I wanted to plant tomatoes. I have no idea how they got there. Probably some squirrel did the mischief, reburying the bulbs as food for the winter. When Lydia saw me, shovel in hand, ready to prepare the soil for this year's planting, she threatened me with dire consequences if I dug up those tulips. I reluctantly put away my shovel, and now I bless Lydia for it. I can't help but admire their contrasting colors and their foolish resilience.

Who Defines the Weeds?

My friend Paul's biodiverse ecosystem philosophy is not easily translated into church life. His "let the weeds be" ideals are too messy and uncontrollable. But our Scriptures reflect the tension between order and chaos, between monoculture and biodiversity. The struggle for most church communities is dealing with a proliferation of people and ideas, deciding what to do with what it sees as weeds. What should the extent of its hospitality be to people who aren't really kin?

The Bible itself reflects the ongoing tension between tending a clean, productive garden, and letting some bright colors spring up among the green. I'm intrigued by the radically contradictory visions of Ezra and Isaiah. Their methods are so different that it raises the question of whether we can keep Isaiah and Ezra in the same Bible. For that matter, can you and I stay in the same church?

In chapter 55 of Isaiah, the prophet speaks of Israel's homecoming from exile in Babylon. The Babylonians had conquered Jerusalem in 586 BC, and large numbers of Jews had been dragged into exile into Babylon. But now the exile is ending. The people of Judah can go home after seventy years in captivity.

Isaiah 55 resonates deeply with me and is one of my favorite texts of Scripture. It invites everyone who thirsts to "come to the waters" (verse 1) and "seek the Lord while he may be found" (verse 6). In an outburst of poetic exultation, Isaiah shouted, "For you shall go out in joy, and be led back in peace; the mountains and the hills before you shall burst into song, and all the trees of the field shall clap their hands" (verse 12).

But then reality sets in for the returning exiles. It's truly wonderful to be going home, but the euphoria of homecoming and images of an idealized holy city can carry them only so far. They have to deal with organizing life again in a difficult environment. Jerusalem isn't going to be much of a home at first. It has been mostly destroyed and is an awful, barren mess, filled with poverty and despair and little rule of law. Strangers are living there, people who moved in to fill the void and occupy abandoned homes. They will probably dispute the exiles trying to lay claims to land on which occupants have lived for seventy years. Most of the original exiles have died; those returning were born in Babylon. For the returnees Judah is a foreign land, known only through the traditions and stories of their elders.

When the exiles arrive home, two visionaries, Isaiah and Ezra, try to bridge the seven-hundred-mile gap between Babylon and Jerusalem. They spell out competing visions of how to organize their community life.

Ezra's Vision

After returning "home" to Jerusalem, the Jewish leader Ezra is deeply troubled. The exiles are trying to re-form their faith community, but he recognizes the threat of assimilation with the pagans who have flooded the land. The returning exiles' identity as God's people, as a people of covenant, is fragile. What do you do when your very identity as a distinct community is threatened by assimilation, when it looks like you might be absorbed into the general mass of pagan society? Ezra hears the complaint of his officials:

> "The peoples of Israel, the priests, and the Levites have not separated themselves from the peoples of the lands with their abominations. . . . For they have taken some of their daughters as wives for themselves and for their sons. Thus the holy seed has mixed itself with the peoples of the lands." (Ezra 9:1-2)

Ezra holds a census and discovers that many Jews, especially the leaders, have in fact married alien women (see Ezra 10). He prays a long, impassioned prayer of repentance and demands that the people get rid of these foreign wives. Most of the assembly agrees, but "Jonathan son of Asehel and Jahzeiah son of Tikvah opposed this, and Meshullam and Shabbethai the Levites supported them" (10:15). But the opposition to Ezra's vision seems to have had little impact. The last verse in the book says simply, "All these had married foreign women, and they sent them away with their children" (10:44). They were excluded from the community being newly formulated and established in Jerusalem.

Ezra's vision made sense in his context. The threat of assimilation into a foreign culture and religion was real. The community's identity as a chosen people of Yahweh God was precarious. Sometimes you need to look to the outer perimeters of your sense of peoplehood and close the porous boundaries that let in those who threaten your identity and purity.

To our modern sensibilities, such an action seems extreme. Send away all the foreign wives with their children? What about the women who married foreign husbands? They aren't mentioned, but perhaps they were already excluded.

Isaiah offers an alternate, even competing, vision.

Isaiah's Vision

Isaiah 56 spells out a vision for rebuilding the covenant community after the return from exile. Isaiah claims that this vision comes from the Lord.

> Thus says the Lord: Maintain justice, and do what is right, for soon my salvation will come, and my deliverance be revealed. Happy is the mortal who does this, the one who holds it fast, who keeps the Sabbath, not profaning it, and refrains from doing any evil. (56:1-2)

This vision begins with fundamentals as old as Abraham (see Genesis 18:19) and revisited by prophet after prophet. The basis of God's community needs to be "justice and righteousness" (see Amos 5:7, 24; 6:12). There is an ethical center to being God's people.

Living ethically and anticipating fuller salvation is rooted in keeping the Sabbath. Keeping the Sabbath is a sign that you have faith that God is working and that you don't have to make it all come out right. You can rest because God, not you, is Lord of the world. You can break the cycle of competitive production and consumption, and just rest and worship. The theme of the Sabbath will return as central to Isaiah's vision of who should be included in the reconstituted community. The specifics of his vision come with stunning, controversial force.

> Do not let the foreigner joined to the Lord say, "The Lord will surely separate me from his people"; and do not let the eunuch say, "I am just a dry tree." For thus says the Lord: To the eunuchs who keep my sabbaths, who choose the things that please me and hold fast my covenant, I will give, in my house and within my walls, a monument and a name better than sons and daughters; I will give them an everlasting name that shall not be cut off.
>
> And the foreigners who join themselves to the Lord, to minister to him, to love the name of the Lord, and to be his servants, all who keep the sabbath and do not profane it, and hold fast my covenant—these I will bring to my

holy mountain, and make them joyful in my house of prayer; their burnt offerings and their sacrifices will be accepted on my altar. (56:3-7)

Who will be included and who will be excluded? Who will be an insider and who an outsider? Isaiah's vision is shockingly inclusive, especially given the context of chaos, confusion, and struggle with the many foreigners who had inhabited Jerusalem. Ezra and others are setting boundaries, putting up fences, and purifying membership lists, but Isaiah sets out to include all people.

Among those Isaiah specifically cites are the eunuch and the foreigner, whom Moses himself excluded. As Deuteronomy 23:1-6 states,

> No one whose testicles are crushed or whose penis is cut off shall be admitted to the assembly of the Lord. Those born of an illicit union shall not be admitted to the assembly of the Lord. Even to the tenth generation, none of their descendants shall be admitted to the assembly of the Lord. No Ammonite or Moabite shall be admitted to the assembly of the Lord.

By admitting the eunuch and the foreigner, Isaiah is apparently moving beyond the boundaries set by Moses, welcoming those Ezra took pains to exclude.

To determine who should be welcomed into the community, Isaiah offers criteria that have accountability built in. Those the Lord includes "keep my Sabbath . . . and hold fast my covenant." These precepts are the center of faith: Keep the Sabbath. Acknowledge that your own efforts to make a go of life aren't enough; you need to rest and depend on God, who is working for you. Hold fast to the covenant. Commit yourself to a relationship of trust in God. Acknowledge the salvation God has brought. Respond by keeping the commandments. It doesn't matter that you are a eunuch or a foreigner. What matters is that you keep the Sabbath and hold fast the covenant. (See Walter Brueggemann's *Using God's Resources Wisely: Isaiah and Urban Possibility* [Westminster John Knox Press, 1993]).

The Tension

I confess that I'm drawn more to the not-so-clean garden vision of Isaiah than I am to the weed-free vision of Ezra. It seems to me that Jesus quotes Isaiah more than he quotes Ezra, including a major quotation from Isaiah 56. After saying that the foreigner who keeps the Sabbath and holds fast to God's covenant will be "joyful in my house of prayer," Isaiah states, "for my house shall be called a house of prayer for all peoples. Thus says the Lord God, who gathers the outcasts of Israel, I will gather others to them besides those already gathered" (verses 7-8). Jesus quotes this text when he cleanses the temple.

Ezra and Isaiah stand side by side as biblical prophets, and their respective visions exist side by side in the church today. Should we eliminate one or the other, or do they each offer a necessary corrective? Are they meant to exist side by side in creative tension? (I explored some of these thoughts in an article entitled "Can we keep Isaiah and Ezra in the same Bible, and you and me in the same church?" in *Vision: A Journal for Church and Theology*, Spring 2002, p. 25-33.)

Every human community makes decisions about who belongs and who doesn't. Always there will be insiders and outsiders. Consider ceremonies in which Canadian citizenship is bestowed on immigrants.

Emmanuel came to Canada from India. It took him many years working and a stringent application process before he was deemed acceptable for Canadian citizenship. Tellingly he became a member of our church long before he became a citizen. It was easier for him to become a member of the church than a citizen of Canada. Emmanuel's face was beaming that day as he proudly sang "Oh, Canada." He invited a number of us to an Indian restaurant to celebrate his new citizenship. He was still Indian, but now he was fully Canadian as well. He was finally an insider, and that needed to be celebrated.

Recently our media have been full of stories of Portuguese "illegals" who are being deported from Canada. This is creating a labor shortage, because the Portuguese perform essential services in Canada's construction industry. They are hard-working and law-abiding people, but they haven't followed all the rules. So even though we need them and find little fault with them, we're obliged to deport them. They cannot become insiders unless they follow proper procedures. They are hoed down as undesirable weeds.

The *Toronto Star* carried a story on April 29, 2006, ("Immigration Seizes Girl to Lure Parents" by Isabel Teotonio) about immigration officials going to a Toronto school to seize two children, threatening to take them from their parents, who were from Costa Rica, if the parents did not turn themselves in within thirty minutes. The parents had overstayed their welcome, and Canada was so desperate to keep her garden clean that children had to be seized and threatened.

The church struggles with drawing lines between insiders and outsiders, but I hope overzealous Canadian immigration officials are not our model. Canada does need to have criteria for citizenship; we would lose the sense of what it means to be Canadian if there were not a common set of identity markers, whether that be our national anthem, our flag, our history, our maple leaf, or even "hockey night." The church also needs criteria for membership, a common set of identity markers. There has to be something that focuses what it means to belong, to be a member. There has to be something that identifies us as being fruit or vegetable, thus belonging in the garden and not in the field with the grain. This implies nothing against grain, but grain isn't vegetable.

Our garden has boundaries that identify it as a garden and not a field. Though it's open on one side with room for expansion and growth, the garden has a "centering" focus on growing only fruits and vegetables.

Jake

Our flight back to Toronto from Vancouver had a stopover in a small Canadian city. Lydia and I decided to go for a walk outside the terminal while we waited. I vaguely noticed that we passed some cars waiting to pick up passengers in a designated waiting area. We had just returned to the terminal when a man from one of those cars rushed up to me and said, "You're Gary Harder, aren't you?"

"Yes," I responded. "I am Gary Harder. But I don't think I recognize you."

"I'm Jake. We used to go to your church. Don't you remember?"

Twenty years earlier, Jake and his wife had come to church periodically but remained on the edges of our congregation. What was regular about them was that every four or five months their marriage hit a crisis. Then they would call me. This went on for some years in a predictable pattern, in a repeating cycle of anger, spiteful acts, and deliberately hurting each other. Their two children suffered greatly. I tried to use my training in pastoral counseling, but to little effect.

One day they came to my office again in total crisis. I had had enough. I still don't know if my anger got the best of me or if it was actually the Holy Spirit working in unconventional ways, but I yelled at them.

I've never yelled at anyone, before or since. Yelling at them violated everything in my training and theology. In high decibels I shouted, "You come in here regular as clockwork, every few months, with your marriage in tatters, begging for help. But you never listen to what I say. You never do anything to change. You know what you need to do to fix things, but you refuse to do it. Three months from now you'll be knocking on my door again. Well, I'm sick and tired of it. I'm sick and tired of you. I refuse to talk to you again. Get out of my office and don't come back. You need to stop doing such stupid things. You need to stop being so damned selfish. You need to turn your life completely over to Christ. Now get out of here and don't come back until you change your lives."

The couple left, fuming, and never came back to church. I heard indirectly that they also left the city shortly after and moved to another province. I heard nothing more from them until Jake rushed up to me in the terminal.

It seems the Holy Spirit was active after I completely lost my composure. Now Jake greeted me warmly. He told me that he and his wife both had experienced a profound spiritual change, the beginnings of which occurred there in my noisy office. With this new center in their lives, their marriage was reborn. Its boundaries were now secure, not breached anymore. He proudly showed me pictures of the two of them and of his two children and four grandchildren. Their messed-up kids were both baptized on confession of faith, and both have good marriages and good jobs.

Now God had brought them into my life again in a chance encounter during a layover at an airport. I still feel guilt for how I yelled at them—but profoundly grateful to the Holy Spirit, who used even my emotional outburst to help bring about transformation.

Dancing Through Thistles in Bare Feet

I've been surprised by how often my reflections have grown out of my farming background. I suppose that in my very being there's a strong link between *pastoral*, meaning rural, and *pastoral*, describing the life of a minister. Certainly my background offers many metaphors for my occupation, especially around issues like boundaries, weeds, disease, and insiders and outsiders. Now a new and deeply personal metaphor splashes across my consciousness.

As a youngster I could have been nicknamed Shoeless, because all summer I ran around barefoot, resistant even to wearing shoes to church. Being barefoot all summer I developed thick calluses on the bottoms of my feet. I could run anywhere without much discomfort, even on thistles or gravel. While I was nearly immune to pain from the many things I stepped on, there were exceptions.

Twice I stepped on nails protruding from boards. Both times the nail was imbedded deep into my foot and had to be wrenched out. My parents feared disease or infection, but my foot healed, and I continued to run carelessly without shoes. Once while picking raspberries, I stepped on a bee. Its stinger penetrated my calluses, and my whole foot swelled painfully.

I loved the freedom of running unencumbered by shoes. I felt like I was dancing through a meadow, oblivious to pricks and barbs, thistles and stones. But my feet weren't the only part of me that developed calluses.

I also grew some thick skin around my emotions. I didn't let much penetrate my heart or mess with my feelings. I really thought that I didn't have a temper, that I was even-tempered and fully in control of my emotions. Positive feelings were okay. Negative feelings didn't penetrate my consciousness.

I thought I could run through pastoral work with a smile on my face. I thought I would be able to manage anything people threw my way, no matter how barbed it might be. I was almost unaware of the impending crisis in my professional life and in my marriage. Trying to be only positive all the time in my relationships was a recipe for shallowness, for superficiality, for triviality. Lydia sensed the crisis in our marriage long before I did, but she wasn't able to articulate it.

Though I was sure I was in control of my life and my future, God intervened. Because of my earlier experiences with pastoring, I was focused on becoming a better pastor and learning how to offer pastoral care. I thought I had a good handle already on interpreting Scripture and thinking theologically. By the middle of my second year at seminary, I was exploring the best way to gain this practical knowledge.

An opportunity came to do a year of pastoral internship at Valleyview Mennonite Church in London, Ontario. I read the information sheets carefully. I would spend time within the congregation in supervised preaching, teaching, and pastoral care. But I would also do chaplaincy work at the London Psychiatric Hospital, in a nursing home, in a home for recovering alcoholics, and in a home for troubled teens. Each of these assignments would be supervised. There was also a unit of clinical pastoral education at the psychiatric hospital, where I would be involved in a small peer group.

We happily moved to London for the year—and into crisis. I had no idea that the path to learning pastoral "skills" would be a train track running through my guts. My supervisors and peers kept probing into my emotions, not my abilities. Lydia soon realized that as they penetrated my thick, callous emotional skin, I was becoming exhausted from the battle and had little emotional energy, positive or negative, left for my marriage and family. So she entered a spouse's support group led by a psychiatrist at the hospital. Together we also went to a couples small group, and eventually my calluses were penetrated. I felt more raw emotions than I knew existed, and together we experienced emotional intimacies new to us.

That year saved both our marriage and my career as a pastor. But it felt sometimes like I had stepped on a whole board full of protruding nails and been stung by a swarm of killer bees, all because I naively thought I only needed to gain how-to pastoral skills. But I discovered that I needed to be in touch with my emotional life if I was ever to be in touch with my spouse's or anyone else's emotional life, whether of pain or of joy.

I am still sometimes tempted to develop calluses, grow a thick skin, and rely on learned skills. I would rather avoid emotional pain. But then I realize again that pastoring, like any loving, is about relationships. And if these relationships are going to have healing intimacy in them, I will have to enter the full range of human emotions with people, including pain, sometimes despair, and often anger.

I think God intervened in my life back there in London. God gave me an emotional freedom that sent me dancing through the pastoral scene in bare feet. I do step on a lot of stuff. I've got all kinds of burrs in my life and personality that still prick me and others. There are plenty of thorny issues to deal with in the church, as in any human community. Occasionally there are even prickly people who continue to do their porcupine thing.

But I don't want to get all calloused up again. I would rather dance through the thistles in bare feet, feeling all the textures of people's lives. And of my own.

Chapter 5

CONFLICT:

A COMPLICATED UNKINDNESS

We had dinner together that evening in February of 2002, and she told us her story. After a long journey of discovery, Shannon had come to the full awareness that she was lesbian in her sexual orientation. She was now in a dating relationship with another woman and had fallen in love.

Shannon Neufeldt was my associate pastor responsible for youth ministries and had requested a meeting with me and Lydia. I sensed that there was something important she wanted to share with us, but I could not have imagined this. Lydia, who is more sensitive to such matters than I, told me later that she had already anticipated what this was about.

Until 1998, I had been a solo pastor, alone in my office at the church and alone with the pastoral responsibilities for the church. When Shannon came on as my associate, I soon discovered how much I enjoyed team ministry. I appreciated her as a colleague.

Some years earlier I'd been Shannon's supervisor and mentor. Our church has a student minister program in which we invite a young student from Canadian Mennonite University to test a calling to ministry. Each spends the summer with us, experiencing ministry, reflecting on it, and exploring his or her gifts. The fact that we already knew Shannon from her internship with us ten years earlier may have been a factor in hiring her as an associate pastor.

Shannon is a deeply spiritual person with a rich and profound prayer life. Our weekly staff meetings always included a time of praying together. She became a trusted, loved colleague and co-pastor with me. Her spiritual depth translated into a growing gift in leading public worship and in preaching. With appreciation, I watched her worship leading become stronger and stronger. With depth, integrity, and assurance, Shannon helped lead the congregation into God's presence. She also has a good organizational mind. When she arranged things, both the larger plan and the details were taken care of.

But Shannon is also an introvert. She doesn't easily "glad-hand" people with a handshake and a smile. For those who were her pastoral responsibility, especially the youth, this introversion didn't matter because she had the time to develop long-term relationships. But many in our congregation didn't really get to know her, apart from her limited public persona.

When my colleague told us that she was in love with a woman, I knew that our congregation would be divided in response to her story. The Mennonite Church was having a hard time processing the issue of homosexuals in the church, and I suspected that Shannon's story would unleash powerful dynamics within our congregation and our conference—and probably within me.

I had taken many years to try to arrive at my own personal, theological, and biblical response to homosexuality. I knew a number of Christian gay people. I knew same-sex couples who'd lived together many years in loving, monogamous, healthy relationships. Some of the students in the course Lydia and I taught at Conrad Grebel University College named themselves homosexuals. They carried deep pain and scars from their experience in the church, because they felt rejected by it. In the end they knew that their sense of calling from God to ministry in the church could not yet be fulfilled.

I was not satisfied that I had worked through all the biblical and theological issues around homosexuality. In my mind, the definitive work on this has not yet been done.

At the end of our dinner conversation, Shannon asked me pointedly, "Can you, Gary, knowing that I am queer, accept me as a pastor?"

"If and when I need pastoral care," I answered, "I want someone who can lead me into the presence of God. What is important to me is that person's openness to God's Spirit, not their sexual orientation. We have prayed together many times. I would still trust you as my pastor."

But that didn't mean that I had no turmoil in my soul. Many fears gripped me: fear that the congregation would be polarized because of her "coming out"; fear of what would happen to Shannon; fear of what would happen to me. I wasn't particularly worried about my job or career; since I was approaching retirement, this was less and less a concern. Some of my younger colleagues in ministry don't feel safe expressing their convictions around this issue. They fear losing their jobs if they do. For me, the consequences I feared were strained relationships with people I love and some people's loss of trust in my pastoral leadership. I was aware that I might become the center of conflict in parts of our larger Mennonite constituency as well.

Theoretically I had made my peace with conflict in the church. Conflict is an inevitable part of any human community. The important issue is not whether we have it, but how we deal with it. But I never welcome conflict.

I also experienced some anger: anger with Shannon for not allowing me to share in her long journey of discovery; anger with our culture and the wider church for making such a big issue of something that is not a big issue in the Bible; anger with myself for being in emotional turmoil and for not having a road map for processing the next months in our congregation.

The emotional meter on this issue is on high red when, in my opinion, it hardly registers as an important issue in the Scriptures, and I resented all the time, energy, and emotion that would be required in the coming long process. I worried that we would become a "one issue" church, and I felt it would be a distraction from the many exciting things happening among us.

Though I worried some, I really thought our congregation would manage a healthy process of discernment and maintain a conversation throughout because we were so used to agreeing and disagreeing with respect. As the seasoned pastor who knew his congregation, I could surely shepherd this thing through. Maybe God was choosing us for this exploration so that we could become a model for how to do it right.

I realized later that I was actually far too naively optimistic and arrogant. This was the most intensely conflicted time of my entire pastoral ministry, and here I want to tell my story, not our church's story or Shannon's story. (Shannon tells hers in the book *The Cost of Truth: Faith Stories of Mennonite and Brethren Leaders and Those Who Might Have Been*, edited by Roberta Showalter Kreider, Strategic Press, 2004.) The story I tell is not at all objective, and many people in my congregation will disagree with my perspective. They may in fact be angered by it. But these are my reflections and my emotional journey through a difficult but exciting and opportunity-filled time.

The "Systems Theory" Mantra

"Be a nonanxious presence" is the mantra of systems theory. A nonanxious presence is the most important role for a leader when a group of people becomes uptight and chaos looms. Every human system, whether family, community, church, or workplace, becomes anxious when change is imminent. But change is inevitable, so how does a leader help a system navigate change? By resisting the temptation to be infected by the panic and to respond in a nonanxious way. But how can a pastor stay nonanxious when he knows that all hell is about to break loose and he's about to walk straight into chaos and confusion?

That's when I go jogging. I have been a jogger for more than thirty years. Three or four times a week I run nearly four miles. As an introvert, I like to jog alone. It's my time to be away from people and to close in on myself. Many times I simply enjoy the world I encounter as I pass by. Sometimes I'm oblivious to that world. At times I jog to relieve stress. At other times, jogging reveals stress I didn't know I was carrying. Sometimes I meditate and pray, or I daydream about a pleasanter world. Sometimes I try to sort things out in my head and in my heart.

After Shannon "came out" with Lydia and me, I needed badly to go jogging. I wasn't at all nonanxious. My emotions were all over the map. I didn't know the way ahead. My associate pastor wanted to tell her story to the entire congregation, and I knew that would unleash turmoil. I had to quiet my own heartbeat.

There were also two basic decisions I felt I needed to make. One seemed easy enough: How does a church make decisions in a situation like this? The other I would revisit and question many times: What is my role as pastor? The two are related, of course, but the answer to the first was more obvious to me than the answer to the second.

A cold February wind was blowing as I jogged. Slippery ice patches hid under the light snow that had fallen. The ice you can't see is the most dangerous, no matter what journey you're on.

Question 1: Whose Responsibility Is It Anyway?

It was clear to me that the responsibility for processing Shannon's story and for deciding what must be done about it was not mine alone. As pastor I would not and could not decide her future with us. Nor could our conference leaders. Our understanding of church is that the local congregation takes on its full share of responsibility in consultation with the broader church.

Mennonites have rejected hierarchical systems of power and authority, though we sometimes revert to them. That rejection is traceable to the Anabaptist movement's suspicion of the power of religious authorities back at its founding in the sixteenth century. Anabaptists and other reformers like Luther, talked about the "priesthood of all believers." Every Christian had direct personal access to God, and any believer could be "priest" to any other believer. Anabaptists applied this to mean that every person in the congregation could interpret the Scriptures under the guidance of the Holy Spirit. The congregation as a whole needed to struggle together to try to understand the will of God when decisions had to be made. The pastor could lead and guide but could not exert power over the congregation or make decisions for it.

My conviction was that Shannon's story needed to go to the whole congregation, not just to me or our church leaders. The congregation would need to process the story and discern how to respond to both Shannon and to homosexuals in the church generally. Doing this with integrity would require a great deal of time, education, and discussion.

Many voices in our wider constituency and within our congregation questioned this basic understanding of church and of where responsibility lay for the decision making that needed to happen. Voices on one side said, "Someone in authority needs to exert proper leadership, fire Shannon, and spare us further confusion. After all, our conference has a confession of faith that reserves marriage for a man and a woman. We must abide by that confession. Either our conference leaders should remove Shannon or you as pastor should. We don't need a congregational process to do that." From the other side, voices said, "This is the time for you as pastor to be prophetic. This is clearly a justice issue. Put on your righteous prophet robe and use your power as pastor to declare that Shannon will continue to be our pastor, end of story."

I felt I did not have the power or the authority to do what either of those voices demanded.

Question 2: What Is the Role of the Pastor?

I struggled far more with this question and often second-guessed my answer. The struggle was primarily around two options. As pastor, should my commitment be primarily to an outcome, or should it be primarily to a healthy process. Should I be a facilitator or a prophet? It seemed to me that if I were committed to an outcome, I could subvert and betray the process. On the other hand, if I were committed primarily to a process, would that be a betrayal of a desired outcome and of a person I loved? In the end I decided that my primary role was to try to ensure a good process, not a specific outcome. But when the process broke down in the end, I questioned everything again.

Most of the congregation knew my stance on hospitality to persons of diverse sexual orientation. In a September 13, 1999, article in our denominational periodical, the *Mennonite Reporter* ("In Conversation: Church Membership Begins with God's Acceptance"), I had advocated for church acceptance of Christians who are homosexual. This meant that some people in our congregation wouldn't fully trust my process leadership and would think that I wanted to predetermine the outcome. Others expected me to advocate for Shannon to remain as our associate pastor; they were disappointed and angry that I didn't do this strongly enough.

I'm conscious that despite our Mennonite rejection of hierar-chical power, as pastor I still had considerable power, more than was healthy for the congregation or for me. I didn't want to abuse this power, and I didn't want to silence any voices. But what about my convictions that homosexuals need to be embraced with love and not rejected? Do I put these convictions aside for the sake of a good process? That is a hard, hard question.

In the end, my role was to be a pastor to the entire congregation. I'm a pastor to the congregation as a system and must try to attend to the health of the entire system. In my opinion the system is health-iest when it meets conflict directly and when minority voices aren't driven underground by a leader's exertion of power. I'm also pastor to each person in the congregation. I'm pastor to those who feel strongly that Shannon should be released as our associate pastor and to those who feel just as strongly that Shannon should be retained. This too, in my mind, required a facilitator.

Having chosen, for better or worse, to be committed to a healthy process, it followed that the congregation, not its leaders, had the responsibility to make major decisions. If I have a theolo-gy of the church that insists that the congregation is the most imme-diate context for decisions around church membership and leader-ship, logically it then follows that the congregation's leaders, includ-ing its pastor, must take on the role of facilitating and empowering the congregation for its task. While my head was convinced that this should be my role, my heart continued to have doubts. It would require many miles of jogging to keep some semblance of perspec-tive—and to keep encroaching anxiety at bay.

Paul and the Early Church's Biggest Crisis

Acts 15 is a pivotal chapter in the story of the early church. Its outcome would determine the very identity of the church: would it be restricted to Jewish Christians or will Gentile followers of Jesus be allowed in? The story is filled with great controversy, messy con-flict, and emotionally charged meetings. I suspect that bringing Jews and Gentiles together was even more viscerally charged than bring-ing heterosexuals and homosexuals into the same church today.

The early church had become polarized, and there was a great deal of dissension. Lined up on one side were those who had the Scriptures squarely on their side and insisted that Gentiles could be saved only if they were circumcised, which was, after all, the law of Moses. That was the tradition, and they trumpeted the fact that they had scriptural authority supporting them.

On the other side were folks like Paul, Barnabas, and Peter, who said they had the Holy Spirit on their side. They had seen what the Holy Spirit had done in the lives of Gentiles and were convinced they belonged in the church and should be able to enter without being circumcised. Naming their experience, they could argue that the Holy Spirit was leading them to welcome into the church Gentiles who didn't fulfill all the scriptural laws.

Acts 15 describes the church's highly politicized fight. My picture of Paul is not that of the laid-back, wisely reflective, nonanxious leader. I see in him the fiery prophet. The story as told in Acts suggests that Paul, Barnabas, and Peter were essentially in agreement on everything, but this may be a simplified, even sanitized, version of the story. In Galatians 2 Paul railed against his opponents in that battle, saying that some of them were "false believers secretly brought in, who slipped in to spy on the freedom we have in Christ Jesus, so that they might enslave us" (verse 4). Then he had some harsh words for Peter, who was on his side. According to Paul, Peter had become afraid of the "circumcision party" and was backing away from his convictions. "I opposed him to his face, because he stood self-condemned," (verse 11) Paul insisted. He also had a falling out with his other companion, Barnabas; "the disagreement became so sharp that they parted company" (Acts 15:39).

Talk about a volatile conflict—and a volatile leader! Paul was probably not the best example of the "nonanxious presence" facilitating a thoughtful and respectful discussion. He's not a model for the pastoral role I chose. He would probably have no patience for my commitment to process over outcome.

The Congregation Is Entrusted with Shannon's Story
Shannon told her story to the congregation on Sunday, April 28, 2002. We had agreed that she would take our "sharing our joys and concerns" prayer time following the sermon to inform the

congregation of her journey and discovery around her sexual identity. She named this discovery as part of her spiritual journey. That morning Shannon said, in part,

> I realized that the trouble in my relationship with God was not primarily stagnation, but rather there was something blocking our relationship. Once I noticed and recognized this difference, thoughts from my sub-conscious slowly came to the surface through each session with my spiritual director. These were unbidden thoughts about my own sexuality. Opening myself up to God was forcing me to admit fears that I might be attracted to women. When I could acknowledge even this possibility, I began to be able to pray again and my relationship with God slowly began to deepen. . . . I began to fear the repercussions this could have. . . . I feared rejection from God. That same morning, though, I heard the "voice" of God as clearly as I ever have telling me, "Shannon, you are a child of mine and I love you. I will always love you, no matter what else happens." I knew too that I loved God and my relationship with God was strong enough to withstand whatever might lie ahead.

A small group of church leaders had tried to prepare for that morning. We had drawn in our caring team, our personnel committee, and several leaders from Mennonite Conference of Eastern Canada. We had also brought in an outside consultant. We all felt that the congregation needed to hear the story directly from Shannon. The only venue that made this possible was a Sunday-morning worship service. This decision was challenged by a number of people who felt that Shannon's story was too disruptive of worship and that the children present should have been spared hearing it.

This leadership group also prepared a general plan for hearing the congregation's response. We wanted to assure the congregation that we were trying to put in place forums for them to respond to the story they had just heard. Following Shannon's story, I responded, in part,

Shannon tells her story to us as a Christian person, but also as a Christian pastor. Each of us has our own response to that story told. Our feelings may be intense. . . .

And now something about our process from here on. . . . Shannon invites anyone to speak with her directly. We want to dialogue with each other openly and directly, thus avoiding all gossip and rumor. . . .

We are planning two open public meetings for a fuller opportunity to talk with each other. . . . We are naming this first phase "A season of sharing the story, of responding, of listening to each other and of caring for each other." We want to listen and care for each person in our congregation—including Shannon.

We have thought that there also need to be further steps. We have talked about "A season of education and teaching and learning and praying," a time for some thorough work on biblical, theological, and contemporary perspectives around the subject of homosexuality.

A third phase might be "A season of discernment and decision making." As a congregation we will want to formulate some kind of informed and faithful proposal or response that will help guide our thinking and our actions in light of the story shared.

All of these seasons have to be filled with prayer. Please pray. Pray for Shannon. Pray for yourself. Pray for TUMC. Pray that we will discern God's Spirit.

I'm not sure whether anyone actually heard me after hearing Shannon. Reading now what I said then, the words sound so rational. My emotions that morning were far from rational. I could read the shock on many faces, and I knew the responses would range all over the emotional map. I felt mixtures of emotions too. On the one hand, I admired Shannon for her courage and her calm, centered demeanor while sharing her story. On the other hand, I could feel the emotional intensity loosed in the congregation, and I was afraid of that turmoil. I was also excited by the fact that now we would no longer be able to avoid a deep struggle with an issue so difficult for the church to deal with. But I was also afraid of what might happen to Shannon and the congregation.

Yet I also felt a certain Holy Spirit calmness. I felt that God was indeed present with us. Was this all delusion, a part of my naive overconfidence? At the end of the morning, my prayer was,

> Gracious God, the one who knows each of us by name, the one who looks deep within each heart, the one who made each of us in your image and loves each human being, love each of us in a special way this morning. Come with your compassion to each aching heart.
>
> At the best of times we struggle to know who we are, to come to terms with who we are, and still to love ourselves. At the best of times we struggle to understand and come to terms with our own identity and our own sexuality. Today Shannon has shared with this congregation that she is a lesbian, that that is who she is, that that is the way she has been created. She has shared her story with great courage and with great pain. Continue to hold her in your loving hand.
>
> We who have heard her story also feel deep emotional things, perhaps feelings we still can't articulate. We know that this story will affect us deeply, as individuals and as a congregation. We know that emotions will vary greatly across our congregation. Continue to hold each one of us in your loving hand.
>
> And so we enter a journey with Shannon and with each other and with you, O God. But there doesn't seem to be a road map for this one; the way ahead is not clear to us. We implore your guidance. We implore your presence. We implore your Holy Spirit to attend and lead us.
>
> Gracious God, continue to call each of us by name, to look within each heart, and to love each of us with your healing love. Amen.

As I reflect on that prayer now, it seems that I was trying to hold together my love for Shannon with my love for the congregation, and I was fearing that this might tear all of us apart.

Cornelius Enters the Story

Cornelius was a Gentile. He entered the Jewish/Christian story and unleashed a huge conflict. At the time, there was great animosity between Gentiles and Jews; each had rigid stereotypes of the other. Paul rattled off the Jewish stereotype of Gentiles in Romans 1.

> Since they did not see fit to acknowledge God, God gave them up to a debased mind and to things that should not be done. They were filled with every kind of wickedness, evil, covetousness, malice. Full of envy, murder, strife, deceit, craftiness, they were gossips, slanderers, God-haters, insolent, haughty, boastful, inventors of evil, rebellious toward parents, foolish, faithless, heartless, ruthless. (verses 28-31)

The fascinating part here is that Paul seems to include both Gentile and Jew in this description. Idolatry, the root sin, can be found in both peoples (John E. Toews, *Romans*, Believers Church Bible Commentary, Herald Press, 2004, p. 71).

Apparently Cornelius didn't fit the sinner stereotype at all. According to the description in Acts 10, "he was a devout man who feared God," prayed, and was generous to the poor he met on the streets. For some reason an angel came to him and told him that "Your prayers and your alms have ascended as a memorial to God" (verse 4). That is a bit of a shock to us, his being neither Jewish nor Christian. Oh, and he was also a military man. For us Mennonites, convinced pacifists, that comes as an extra shock. And still his prayers are answered?

God wanted Cornelius the Gentile to meet Peter, a Jewish follower of Jesus. Such things shouldn't happen. The New Testament seems to mess around with certitudes quite a lot. On the one hand, the New Testament makes clear statements that Jesus is the way to God, such as, "Jesus said . . . , 'I am the way, and the truth, and the life. No one comes to the Father except through me'" (John 14:6). Story after story is told of people who don't know Jesus and who aren't Jews, but who have faith that's pleasing to God. Jesus himself said to a Roman centurion who asked for the healing of a servant that he had more faith than anyone in Israel (see Matthew 8:5-13). It can all be very, very unsettling.

God answered the prayers of Cornelius, whatever they were, in a terrifying way—assuredly not in the way he was praying for. The angel told him that God had a new vision for him, one that would make his life and his faith fuller and more complete. But he would need to send for Simon Peter, the Jew who became a Jesus follower, to find it. Terrified as he was, Cornelius sent one of his soldiers and two slaves to look for Peter. He was being prepared to enter the Jesus story (verse 8).

The Leadership Team

The congregation selected a leadership team to guide our discernment process. It needed to be a representative team, reflecting the convictions of a cross section of the congregation. The five members of the team, plus me as *ex officio* member, covered the entire spectrum of opinion and conviction on the issue. "Can this work?" I wondered. "Or is the team's makeup a guarantee for infighting and polarized paralysis?"

We met together, hesitant, fearful, overwhelmed, not knowing if we could trust each other. We started slowly, each of us sharing where we were personally on the issue right then and what our dreams and visions and fears were about working together. There was no point playing nice, safe, superficial games with each other. Our job was to put our story, our convictions, and our anxieties on the table as honestly as we could.

We were drawn into each story almost against our will. We began to see the issue from each other's perspectives. Amazingly we began to trust each other and were ready to pray together at the end of the evening. Trust grew and deepened throughout the year-and-a-half process as we worked together to guide the church in its discernment. We genuinely enjoyed each other and our meeting times. We struggled hard with our planning and with knowing where to go with the process. But we enjoyed working, studying Scripture, and praying together. It seemed that God was working in and through our diverse group. It felt like a small miracle.

To my mind, the leadership team was a microcosm of what ideally I want the church of Jesus Christ to be: a group of people with radically different or opposite convictions, learning to trust and love each other and work together to discern what it means to follow Jesus today.

Opinions in the congregation about the success of the leadership team varied widely. I don't want to defend the planning we did or negate the mistakes we made. But I do want to celebrate the unity we experienced in the midst of our diversity.

The work was hard, long, and draining, and yet rewarding. One particular meeting stands out in my mind for its sudden, almost giddy humor. For some crazy reason, everything that evening struck us as funny. Puns flowed nonstop. Jokes grew out of every planning strategy. We laughed our way to consensus on the next action steps. Our praying together at the end of the meeting felt almost too lighthearted for such a heavy agenda. We wore smiles through our praying. Because we joked so much, the meeting went later than usual. I arrived home, expecting Lydia to be long asleep. Instead she was waiting up for me.

"Did you laugh a lot at your meeting tonight?" were her first words to me.

"How in the world did you know?" I blurted back.

"Well, Judi and I were thinking about your meeting, and we knew you were all kind of worn out, and we thought that what you needed most was to laugh together. And so we kept praying that God would give you lots of laughter and fun this evening. Did you laugh a lot?"

Our process unfolded. The first period of "listening to each other and caring for each other" had intense times of sharing and naming our fears, our angers, our hopes. There were plenary meetings, small-group meetings, many one-on-one conversations, and a number of opportunities to express what was going on inside of us. We named a long, long list of emotional responses: shock, fear, anger, relief, compassion, love, confusion, betrayal, admiration, awe, exhilaration, sadness, anxiety, pride, heaviness, tiredness. But then summer intervened.

In the fall we launched an intensive six-month "season of learning" about human sexuality. A separate planning group led this teaching-learning time. I felt particularly aware that our congregation had enormous personal gifts and resources for this study time. Because of our location near the universities, and especially the Toronto School of Theology, we had leaders among us on nearly every aspect of our study who were able to guide us through the Old Testament or New Testament, theology, psychology, psychiatry, and other sciences. We didn't ask first where they stood on the issue, only what wisdom and expertise they could offer us. They did, in fact, cover the whole spectrum of conviction and were a very rich offering to our congregation.

Most of the congregation participated in the study, which looked at those texts in the Bible that in some way mention sexual activity. We planned the six months in such a way that, while the Sunday school addressed the issue of human sexuality, preaching during worship focused on how to be church when we disagree with each other.

As a naive optimist, I wasn't anxious during this phase but quite confident. Good things were happening, and we were learning so much. It seemed to me that God was blessing our search. In a sermon called "Now is a time for trusting," I said. "I want to declare my trust in the Scriptures. I want to declare my trust in the Holy Spirit to guide us. I want to declare my trust in the church, both the wider church and this congregation." But I wondered if my trust in the church would be rewarded.

In the midst of this crisis, the year brought eighteen new members—two by baptism and sixteen by transfer of membership. They were people from both sides of the aisle on homosexuality. At our sharing meeting before one membership Sunday, one couple said, "It feels a bit scary joining the church now. We feel so strongly that the church needs to be fully open to gays, and we don't know how the church will decide this one." Another couple countered, "It feels just as scary for us. We feel just as strongly that homosexual activity is condemned by the Bible, and we don't know whether our conviction will be honored by the church." To my surprise, dealing with conflict head-on seemed to attract new members rather than repel them.

Some members of the congregation did not trust the work of the leadership team or the process we planned. They perceived our leadership to be influenced by outsiders from the gay community who were orchestrating an outcome: acceptance of Shannon as pastor of TUMC and full acceptance of homosexuality. Shannon's telling of her story was suspected to be a part of this "gay agenda," which meant, some thought, that we were trying to manipulate an outcome.

Many knew that I was open to Christian homosexuals being fully included in the church. Most knew that I had a strong relationship with Shannon. It was also generally conceded that a majority of the congregation was on the "open" side, which was reason enough for minority voices to feel threatened. Some wondered how I could be objective in leading the process. For me, the raising of the "gay agenda" theory felt like a betrayal of trust in the team and in me as pastor. I felt that my integrity was being questioned, which made me angry. Rationally I understood where the suspicion came from, but I found it unsettling nonetheless.

What About Peter?

Peter was in for a great shock. There had been plenty of them since he'd met Jesus. He had been a fisherman until Jesus asked him to leave the nets behind and follow him. As new traveling companions he had a tax collector, the type of person he despised, and some Zealots, of whom he was afraid. Along the way he developed visions of power and prestige but was told, instead, to be a servant and like a child (see Mark 8:33-37; Matthew 18:4). At one point, Peter blurted out the magnificent confession that he thought Jesus was the Messiah, but it was clear that he didn't understand what kind of messiah Jesus would be. Peter would have none of Jesus' talk of suffering, of being rejected and of being killed, even when Jesus added that he would rise again after three days.

When the soldiers came to arrest Jesus in the garden of Gethsemane, Peter saw his chance to be a hero. He grabbed a sword to defend his master, but Jesus told him to put away the sword (see John 18:10-11). Then came the final ignominy of his cowardice: denying that he knew Jesus at all (see verses 15-27).

But after all that, after Jesus' death and resurrection, after Jesus forgave Peter, and after Pentecost, Peter became a respected leader in the fledgling church. He finally had it all together as a mature, seasoned leader, until he too saw a life-altering vision.

On a journey, Peter fell into a trance. In the trance he was hungry. Soon he saw food coming to him—mounds of animals on a sheet coming out of heaven. But the animals were all unclean and profane to him as a Jew. A voice said it was okay for him to kill the animals and eat them. He protested, because that would defile him, make him unclean. The voice told him that what God made clean, he shouldn't call profane. The dream recurred three times. Still perplexed, Peter met three men who invite him to come to the home of Cornelius, the Gentile. The trance would prepare him for that meeting. (See Acts 10:9-23.)

Life is more orderly when you have good solid rules to follow. The rules of clean and unclean were mostly a good thing; they gave order and identity to being Jewish and clarity about how God wanted the Jews to live a holy life. Peter had obeyed the food laws all his life. Now he was being shown, through a vision, that these laws didn't apply anymore. The gospel of Jesus Christ transcended them, especially because they were a barrier to Gentiles wanting to enter this Jesus movement. Peter would have to give them up to meet Cornelius.

Preparing for a Decision

In April 2003 we began our "season of discernment." I decided to write a pastoral letter to the congregation, explaining my convictions about the issue. I was committed to a healthy process and didn't want to abuse my power or unduly influence the congregation's decision making. I didn't want to be perceived as demanding conformity to my views.

If one part of what I perceived to my pastoral role during this time was to be a nonanxious presence, the other part was to be aware of the power I had as pastor. As a senior pastor who had been in the congregation for fifteen years already, I had accumulated considerable power. This can be healthy and help a group move forward. At its best, it empowers others, especially minority voices, which I wanted to do. But power can easily be abused. A pastor can silence voices that need to be heard.

My struggle was to find a public way to state my convictions without derailing the conversation. The letter would be my opportunity to clarify my own convictions and to process my own under-standing of the theological and biblical issues involved. We'd brought many books and articles from every perspective into the church library that year, along with a number of resource people covering all views. Now I wanted to systematically process it all for myself and share it with the congregation.

My personal integrity demanded this. In the end it was not enough only to be a facilitator of process. I needed to put my con-victions on the line. We asked this of everyone else in the congre-gation, so I needed to ask it of myself.

This was a part of being "self-differentiated" (another systems theory mantra). It made me publicly accountable for my position and beliefs. The question was how to do it while giving the freedom for the debate to continue.

Part of my struggle was realizing that it might jeopardize some relationships. I felt that one of my greatest strengths as a pastor was my relational style. I related fairly easily across a wide spec-trum of people. I knew that stating my convictions clearly and publicly might alienate me from those within our congregation for whom I cared deeply. It would alienate me from people across our denomination. So I couldn't share lightly.

I jogged many extra miles that April. I consulted with the lead-ership team and with our church board. Then I published my let-ter in the hope that by then our seasons of learning and discerning would have provided people with the intellectual framework for processing my views and challenging them if they wished.

Simply stated, my pastoral letter said that the traditional inter-pretations of those Scriptures that mention same-sex sexual activity did not convince me that it should be condemned. The context for those verses indicates violence or rape, as in the case of Sodom and Gomorrah, or an understanding of "uncleanness" according to the Leviticus holiness codes, which we no longer apply to other areas of our lives. Or those verses have to do with male prostitution, with exploitive sex, or with some form of idol worship. I don't see these texts addressing a permanent, loving, committed same-sex relation-ship. I lean much more to a covenantal understanding of marriage, which would leave open the possibility of committed same-sex rela-tionships.

After the letter was published, I felt very vulnerable but also satisfied and relieved deep inside.

Peter and Cornelius Meet

By the time Peter and Cornelius were ready to meet, both had been prepared through unsettling dreams for a new vision bigger than either could imagine. Cornelius had gathered an assembly of relatives and close friends. He was taking this a bit too seriously, perhaps. He was ready to fall down and worship Peter, but Peter assured him that he was only mortal, as were all present, and certainly not to be worshipped. Peter said straight out that, according to Jewish law, he shouldn't be there—associating with a Gentile and entering his home would make him unclean—but God was telling him not to call anyone unclean. So Peter was there without objection (see Acts 10:25-29).

Peter's orientation had been totally altered by the vision he dreamed. His lifelong framework of exclusion was changed. Now he was able to do something he had never done: enter the home of a Gentile and eat with someone he'd always thought would make him unclean and unfit to stand before God. Cornelius responded by saying that those in the house were there to hear what God wanted to say to them. "Preach it, brother."

So Peter began to preach. His shocking opening grabbed the attention of every Gentile, Jew, and Christian: "I truly understand now that God shows no partiality, but in every nation anyone who fears him and does what is right is acceptable to him" (Acts 10:34-35). This was not what Peter was taught at home and in the synagogue. But God was "preaching peace by Jesus Christ—he is Lord of all" (verse 37).

"Let me tell you about this Jesus," Peter might have said. He told his Gentile audience that they were already accepted by God, Gentile though they were, but that their life and their faith would be fuller if they follow Jesus. As Peter preached and they listened, the Holy Spirit worked in the usual mysterious ways. People started speaking in tongues and extolling God. Seeing that the Holy Spirit chose to be poured out even on Gentiles, Peter was ready to baptize them all, and they had a great celebration lasting several days (see verses 44-48).

This story is pivotal in the story of the church. It marks a momentous change of direction. When Peter and his friends went back to Jerusalem and the other Jewish followers of Jesus, they shared the amazing things that had happened in the home of Cornelius. They were roundly criticized for it. "Unless you are circumcised according to the custom of Moses, you cannot be saved" (Acts 15:1). There was such a kafuffle, such a can of worms opened, that they needed to have a whole conference to try to sort it out. The contentious conflict is recorded in Acts 15.

What did Peter see as his pastoral role in that conflict-ridden conference? The report of the conference says that after a debate Peter told the assembly what the Holy Spirit had done in the home of Cornelius. Then he issued a strong challenge: "Now therefore why are you putting God to the test by placing on the neck of the disciples a yoke that neither our ancestors nor we have been able to bear? On the contrary, we believe that we will be saved through the grace of our Lord Jesus, just as they will" (Acts 15:10-11). Very strong words.

What isn't mentioned here is Peter's conflict with Paul. In Galatians 2:11-12, Paul calls Peter a coward. But Peter's Acts 15 speech doesn't sound cowardly at all. I don't know how anxious Peter was during that conference or what fears beset him as he was berated for his new convictions. Was he in the end a coward? The record doesn't say. But the record of this conference indicates that Peter, like Paul, was much more an advocate and a prophet than he was a process facilitator. I can't use either for a model of my chosen stance.

A Lesson Learned Too Late

Our process lurched into the final stages of discernment. By the second of our three long congregational decision-making meetings in June, it felt to me that the process was unraveling and no one in leadership could stop it. I was unraveling too and couldn't stop it.

On our family farm, we had a John Deere model D tractor, which had a flywheel that we had to turn by hand to start the motor. It was hard to turn, especially when the piston valves were closed. Pressure would build up in the pistons when the flywheel was turning, and as a youngster I couldn't start the motor unless I first opened the valves. That released the pressure in great hisses and enabled the engine to start. When the engine was fully started, you closed the piston valves again so that all the pressure could be captured to provide the power to pull the plow.

I don't think we opened the piston valve in our congregational process in time, and it may have been one of our biggest mistakes. We did give opportunity during our season of listening and caring to vent emotional steam, which helped start the engine. But then we moved too much into a rational framework with our season of learning. We probably thought subconsciously that if we fed the mind, our emotions would moderate.

We tried hard to be nice to each other and to speak respectfully, but we probably needed to confront each other sooner and more often. We needed to challenge each other directly and perhaps yell at each other to express our anger and frustration. The emotional pressure built up, but we didn't open the valves and let off steam. The engine was bursting with pressure that had nowhere to go. The flywheel stopped turning. What else could the process do but explode?

What About James?

James was another leader at the Jerusalem conference. The atmosphere was tense as two viewpoints collided head-on. One side agitated for a traditional reading of Scripture in which the law of Moses was paramount. Only circumcision gave entry to the community of faith. "We have to follow the law."

The other group, which included Paul, Barnabas, and Peter, spoke with fiery prophetic zeal. "But see what the Holy Spirit is doing in the lives of Gentiles." Perhaps later, after the conference, Peter may have waffled a bit; as recorded in Galatians 2:11-12. Paul launched a scorching attack on him for no longer being willing to eat with Gentiles. But at this conference he confronted the legalists and declared that the Gentiles will be saved, like the Jews, through the grace of Jesus, not through circumcision. Though this group led by Peter ended up fighting among themselves, at the conference they presented a united front.

The conflict at the Jerusalem conference was sharply stated. I can imagine that emotions were running high. Acts 15:2 says that at a pre-conference meeting there was "No small dissension and debate; the conference itself featured "much debate" (verse 7). Perhaps an open valve had released the high pressure. Everyone had been heard, and the church needed to decide.

Enter James, who seems to have been a voice of moderation. Was his the nonanxious presence? Following a time of silence he spoke as a wise sage bringing together the starting point of both groups. First he affirmed the testimony of Peter. God, through the Holy Spirit, was at work among the Gentiles, quite apart from Jewish law. Then he went to the sacred Scriptures, the starting place for the other side, and interpreted them in light of this new experience.

James quoted the prophet Amos: "So that all other peoples may seek the Lord—even all the Gentiles over whom my name has been called. Thus says the Lord, who has been making these things known from long ago" (Acts 15:17). The Old Testament was illuminated and interpreted by the current activity of God. James challenged one side not to use Scripture as a rigid rulebook, and he challenged the other side to use the Scriptures as a living guide.

In his decision on this matter, James offered a compromise and a new vision. It came in two parts: (1) "We should not trouble these Gentiles who are turning to God" (verse 19). In other words, welcome them into the church without requiring that they first be circumcised. (2) But let's ask them to respect three other important traditions of Moses. Doing that will make it much easier for Jewish Christians and Gentile Christians to eat together: we'll ask them to "abstain only from things polluted by idols and from fornication, and from whatever has been strangled and from blood." These parameters were seen as central to idol worship in the Roman Empire, which was incompatible with following Jesus.

The whole church agreed, and the conflict was over. There was full agreement, so much so that they could say at the end, "It seemed good to the Holy Spirit and to us" (verse 28).

The Worst Congregational Meeting of My Life

We had traditionalists, and we had prophets. But we had no sage like James when the pressure gauge was showing red.

On June 21, 2003, voting took place. We'd had three day-long congregational discernment meetings that June. By the second one, it had become clear to me that we were no longer trying to discern God's will; we were in a political power struggle. The tone of the final meeting before the vote was that of a win-or-lose battle rather than a common search for solutions. It had become political. People came to vote who hadn't been a part of the process or the conversation. The engine was about to explode, and no one knew how to open the valves and release pressure—me included.

What should have been clear to us in leadership was that time had become our enemy. We thought a year-and-a-half process would be enough. We didn't want to keep Shannon in limbo any longer than that. We needed to make a decision about our congregational stance on homosexuality and then whether Shannon could remain in a leadership position. But we weren't spiritually ready that Saturday.

A few voices, primarily women's voices, advised that we postpone the decisions and take time to calm ourselves and keep talking. (It is interesting that when we became political we also became less able to hear the softer voices.) "What's a few more weeks or months?" they asked. Leadership either didn't hear those voices or lacked the wisdom or the courage to stop the process and invite the Holy Spirit back into our discernment.

As pastor I also had the responsibility and perhaps the power to name our descent into power politicking. I could have appealed for more time to find our equilibrium again. But I didn't do that, and I carry guilt for not doing it. More time may not have changed the decisions, but it may have altered the spirit in which we made them.

The decisions we did make that day came in two parts. We passed almost unanimously a statement on human sexuality, including homosexuality, that includes a welcome to homosexuals to worship with us and become a part of our community. The second decision, passed in a close vote, was to release Shannon as our associate pastor. In the end we arrived at an apparent contradiction. On the one hand, we want to be welcoming of persons who are homosexual On the other hand, we released our co-pastor who named herself as lesbian.

I have full respect for deeply held convictions, especially when they're grounded in an understanding of Scripture. I'm convinced that most of our members, whatever their convictions, had based their views on the Scriptures and how they understood the will of God. So I respected both a yes vote and a no vote. The disorientation for me came from how we hurt each other in expressing those convictions. At the end of that meeting I was angry, dispirited, depressed, empty of energy, immobilized, and feeling guilty. It was the worst congregational meeting of my life. I don't think anyone was proclaiming "it seemed good to the Holy Spirit and to us."

At the end of the meeting I confessed to the congregation that "my pastor's heart was broken." I felt immobilized as a pastor. I was disoriented and had stopped being nonanxious. I acknowledged my inability to lead effectively when it was most needed.

I still feel we had engaged in a good and healthy process, but one that ended badly. We'd listened to the Scriptures, to the Holy Spirit, to each other. We'd learned a great deal about human sexuality and about homosexuality. We'd engaged each other honestly and deeply. Many people made themselves vulnerable as they shared their personal stories and convictions. But in the end, it seemed we were all too afraid of what we might lose, and we started to fight with unholy manners.

The issue for me was not primarily the decisions we made. I accepted the will of the congregation, though I grieved Shannon's loss. She was a trusted, appreciated colleague and co-pastor. The breakdown of what had been a dialogical and respectful process was disorientating for me. When it came to crunch time, the congregation couldn't maintain an open engagement with each other. In the end we hurt each other.

Healing Does Come

In August of that year, Lydia and I attended Mennonite World Conference in Bulawayo, Zimbabwe. Every six years Mennonites and Brethren in Christ from around the world gather to celebrate what God is doing among our people. Seven thousand of us, we whites a small minority, gathered daily to engage each other and to worship together. For me the timing of the conference was perfect, a wonderful time for inner renewal.

Part of that renewal was the singing. During the Assembly Scattered week prior to the official conference, Lydia and I took part in a tour of several Brethren in Christ mission stations. We spent three days in Matopo mission, among the magnificent rock formations and ancient caves of the beautiful Matopo hills, where ancient bush people left their drawings. Upon arrival, we were warmly welcomed and taken immediately to the church for evening worship. Suddenly, from within the congregation, a woman began singing, and soon others joined in. A girls choir sang and danced. With rich, deep sounds and harmonies, their rhythms got our whole bodies moving. The twelve girls had stayed behind during their spring break to sing for us, which they did for the next three days. Once, we all sang for over two hours around a campfire. These girls became the soul of our experience at Matopo.

One day we hiked the hills of Matopo, exploring the caves and awe-inspiring rock formations. Massive boulders, one on top of the other, stood at precarious angles. No one could explain how they got there. Maybe it was the work of the Paul Bunyon of Zimbabwe? At a rock they call "the Shoe," our group, plus the twelve girls and the local pastor who was our guide, began to sing as the sun set with breath-taking beauty. The sound echoed magnificently in our rock chamber.

During the conference, Lydia and I stayed with a family in a village outside Bulawayo, which meant a forty-minute bus ride early each morning and late each evening. No sooner would the bus lurch forward than someone would start singing. Soon everyone joined in. The bus throbbed with music and power and life. Always the music was in leader-response style, started by different voices. The passengers became a congregation. We too were part of it, though we didn't understand the Shona words.

At the assembly hall, seven thousand voices sang accompanied by drums, dancing, swaying, clapping, and shouting. Powerful, powerful stuff.

Our gatherings in Bulawayo must have represented one of the most diverse collections of Mennonites and Brethren in Christ imaginable. It was a massive peoplehood from around the world, all committed to Christ, all identified as Anabaptist, yet diverse in culture, language, color, politics, worship styles, and theology. But none of that mattered in the least. We experienced a profound unity in our worship together. We were one in Christ. Period.

Something weighty happened to my spirit in Zimbabwe. I became relaxed and nonanxious about returning to the congregation and dealing with our pain and brokenness.

Some voices within our congregation had said, "Why not just accept the inevitable. We are already a divided congregation. We really do have non-negotiable differences. Let's make it official and split into two congregations. That way we are each with people who agree with us. Then we can each follow our convictions and our ideals, and we don't have to fight with each other anymore."

I realized after Zimbabwe how passionately I disagreed with those voices. I feel that being committed to Jesus and worshipping our living God is such a source of unity that it overshadows all our other divisions, including polarizing convictions.

My commitment then was to a healing journey for myself and the congregation. But some pain cannot be healed. Shannon, her partner, and a few of her close supporters left the congregation; left because of their pain and disillusionment. Maybe they felt as Paul had about Peter, that I had not forcefully enough stated my convictions and had become afraid to be a bold leader. Perhaps they were disillusioned by both the congregation and its pastor.

In Jerusalem

In the early church, the decision that Gentile men could become a part of the church without being first circumcised needed to be communicated to the wider church. After putting that decision down on paper, the leaders selected others to deliver the letters to churches in Antioch, Syria, and Cilicia. The Gentiles in these churches joyfully received the letters. They welcomed the news that they were accepted and seemed content with the few restrictions placed on them.

It was vital to communicate directly and personally with these churches, because other voices were communicating other things. The letter said, in part, "We have heard that certain persons who gave gone out from us, though with no instructions from us, have said things to disturb you and have unsettled your minds" (Acts 15:24). Though the decision had been unanimous, some rumblings continued, and one group was spreading discontent. Resolving conflict seldom satisfies everyone.

We get further hints of discord from Paul's letter to the Galatians. There was some infighting underway. I mentioned earlier Paul's rather harsh-sounding rebuke of Peter. Now James is viewed unfavorably. James was the one who had seemingly mediated the conflict to a happy resolution in the first place. He was the wise man who listened to all sides and came forward with a compromise that seemed to satisfy everyone. His was the nonanxious presence that helped everyone bring together the Scriptures with the new work of the Holy Spirit. But some messiness remained. Paul blamed "certain people who came from James" (Galatians 2:22) for putting pressure on Peter not to eat with Gentiles. Was James himself no longer supporting the compromise he helped forge? Was there some unraveling of the spirit of consensus?

Acts 15 seemed a good model for resolving an issue in a healthy, positive way. There's a great deal to be learned from that story. The early church leaders were human, and conflict continued to be part of their journey.

In Toronto

Our church also communicated its decisions. We wanted to state our outcomes clearly and dispel rumors. Being accountable to the wider Mennonite Church, we thought we might have some valuable lessons to share with other churches struggling with the same agenda. By then we were less arrogant than we had been, humbled and broken in many ways, but we were still trying to be God's people. We wanted to be honest and transparent about our difficult journey.

The electronic media became our primary communication forum. Posting our story and our statement on human sexuality on the Internet felt very impersonal yet also very vulnerable. It didn't result in the universal rejoicing that greeted the letter sent out from Jerusalem. We received a lot of censure for our decisions. There were those upset that we released Shannon and many upset that we included a welcoming invitation to homosexuals in our statement on human sexuality.

Though attending Mennonite World Conference in Zimbabwe that year was healing for me, there would be three more particularly difficult moments for me in the next few months.

August 24, 2003

As I stumbled out of bed, I moaned that this Sunday-morning worship service would be one of the most difficult of my entire ministry. One person from our congregation told me later, "That was the worst worship service I have ever attended." We reached back into the deepest part of the pain of the June meetings and realized how many conflicted feelings we still carried.

That Sunday we were trying to give some closure to our process. We named it a service of lament and confession; we wanted to acknowledge our brokenness and the fact that we had hurt each other.

Even though I was reenergized after Zimbabwe, I still carried the brokenness from our June meetings. I knew I needed to publicly express my broken pastor's heart and confess that I felt immobilized during our decision-making time. My disorientation came less from the seemingly contradictory decisions to be open to homosexuals while removing our associate pastor than from my disappointment that we couldn't be dialogical and respectful even when we were polarized in our convictions. We had deepened our understanding of issues around human sexuality, including homosexuality. We had wrestled seriously with the Scriptures. We had explored our understanding of sexual ethics for Christians. We had struggled with what it means to be the church of Jesus Christ when we disagree fundamentally with each other. But we couldn't maintain open engagement with each other. It seemed we'd turned from searching for the will of God to fighting to make sure our side won.

We needed to lament how we had treated each other and confess our brokenness. On this Sunday, we had gathered the voices of about eighty people from the congregation, and their words were put into a litany of lament. These voices expressed almost every emotion and opinion about what had happened. These were offered to God. The whole service, including my sermon, was structured around the psalms of lament, those that Old Testament scholar Walter Brueggemann called "psalms of disorientation." We named our disorientation.

Earlier that morning, I listened to Bach to quiet my inner turmoil, and I prayed, "God, this is going to be a particularly difficult morning for me and for all of us. Please, we don't want any guests this morning. We don't want to inflict this pain on anyone else."

Either God wasn't listening, or God had in mind to use our lament for healing in other people's lives. There were guests. One man from the neighborhood said later, "If a church can express its pain like you did, and can be so honest, why, that is the kind of community I want to be a part of." He has joined the congregation. A woman came to that service as a first-time visitor. She waited until almost everyone had left the church, then came to me and said, "Pastor, everything that happened in the service today spoke to my heart. I have had so much pain and trauma in my life, and this service is giving me the courage to face it." She too has joined us.

Out of our brokenness, miracles continue to happen. Significant movements toward reconciliation continue, though they are not complete. I have been deeply moved by some of the healing that has happened in my own relationships with people who were very upset with me. Personal convictions around the issue of homosexuality have probably not changed a great deal, but we have all mellowed in how we express them. There is a much freer and easier engagement with each other at this point. We have been able to process follow-up issues with a great deal more respect.

September 21, 2003

I confess that I used my power as pastor when I insisted that we have a full Sunday-morning service of farewell for Shannon. There was little enthusiasm for doing so, but I felt strongly that we needed it, for Shannon's sake, the congregation's, and mine. We had said hello to Shannon four years earlier with many blessings, prayers, and affirmations. What were we to do now to end our covenant with her? Saying goodbye is difficult at the best of times but more so when a rift in the relationship exists.

Difficult as it was, it was healing to hear our young people, one after the other, speak their appreciation for Shannon. It was healing to hear Shannon honestly but graciously speak her farewell. My sense of grief and loss bubbled over because it was a personal loss for me. But for Shannon, I suspect, it was deeper still. It was not only a loss of relationships but also a loss of her people, the Mennonites, and of her calling as a minister within that peoplehood.

When that morning was over I felt empty inside. I felt I had failed both Shannon and the church.

March 2005: A Lesbian Couple Leaves

In March 2005 a lesbian couple left our congregation. Svinda had grown up in TUMC. By the time I arrived in 1987, she was mostly not attending. I assumed the usual teenage issues kept her away from our church but she had also declared herself publicly as a lesbian. I met with her several times over the years, but didn't really know her all that well.

Svinda and her partner, Karin, began attending our church regularly during the middle of the discernment about Shannon. Svinda was in the middle of seminary studies, working on a master's of divinity and planning to follow a call from God into a chaplaincy and counseling ministry or perhaps into pastoral ministry. One of her particular gifts is playing guitar and singing. At various times she drew the congregation into worship with this gift. We also invited her to lead worship several times. She then became a part of our healing and reconciliation team, helping us to work at healing for our broken congregation.

Svinda's partner showed a reflective and deep spiritual faith. She had outgrown some of the narrowness of the tradition in which she had been nurtured and now related easily to a broad spectrum of people. There was a practical bent to her faith. She would quietly offer to bake loaves for communion or help rearrange chairs for a service. To me, this couple modeled the best of a Christian couple, entering the life of a congregation in winsome ways.

One day they asked to see me in my office. My heart was heavy, as I knew intuitively what they wanted to share with me. They said they were leaving TUMC. A letter to the church that Sunday morning expressed frustration with how slowly the congregation was adopting the recommendations of the healing and reconciliation team. They especially wanted the congregation to make some kind of symbolic gesture which would indicate our welcome to homosexuals to worship with us. But the bigger issue was that Svinda knew that she couldn't be ordained as a Mennonite minister. In her studies and vocation she was moving toward ordination, following what she named as her calling from God. I wept with the couple as they left my office.

Jogging and Journeying

The problem with jogging is that you don't get anywhere. It's not a journey. I run the same route over and over again, endlessly repeating my steps. There is no real destination, unless returning home feeling better physically, emotionally, and spiritually is destination enough. The problem with journeying is that you don't always get where you think you want to go—especially when on a spiritual journey where there are no maps.

My jogging gets slower each year. Age is doing that to me, even though speed has never been my strength, either in jogging or in ministry.

My journey with a deeply divided congregation has changed me. I'm less arrogant now, more humbled, and not as naively optimistic. There's a deeper hope in me now too: God has not abandoned us and continues to work in surprising ways. God isn't finished with us yet. We continue to be church and to struggle to find clarity regarding God's will for Christian homosexuals.

In the meantime I continue to jog, and we all continue to journey.

Chapter 6

THREADS:
LIKE A GREAT PEACE FUGUE

From a side balcony, I helped Ivars Taurins conduct, slowed only momentarily when Lydia jabbed me in the ribs. My hands and my body couldn't stop moving. The music weaved through my body and soul. I became a part of the intensity, movement, rhythm, pulse, passion, and dynamism of the performance. I left the Trinity-St. Paul Centre dancing. Transcendence felt closer again.

Bach

It was Wednesday evening, and Lydia and I were attending a performance of the Tafelmusik Baroque Orchestra and Chamber Choir performing Bach's Mass in B Minor. This Mass epitomizes the heart of my love for Bach's music. Though Bach set to music the traditional text of the Catholic Mass, he was a Lutheran, not a Catholic. In this musical setting he created perhaps his greatest legacy.

My soul resonates deeply with the Mass in B Minor, especially on Easter Sunday morning, when its Credo section rings at high volume off our living-room walls. The Credo is the "we believe" section of the Mass, not normally the first place I as a Mennonite would turn to.

Mennonites are not often seen as a creedal people. Our argument with both the Catholics and the Reformers during the Reformation was that creeds, doctrines, and beliefs weren't enough. Reciting the Nicene Creed every Sunday and claiming that you believed in Jesus wasn't enough. What was important was living and embodying our faith by trying to live the way Jesus taught us to live. Central to how we Anabaptists understood following Jesus was his way of love and peace. Following Jesus meant expressing love in all our relationships, even with our enemies, and rejecting any use of violence.

Following Jesus, not just believing, was the key to being a Christian. Among Mennonites there has always been an uneasiness with making creedal formulations, and we aren't inclined to recite the creeds on Sunday morning like many other Christian traditions do. Mennonites have written many confessions of faith, but we don't quite have the weight of "gospel," of an insistence that a person believe everything exactly as written in order to be truly Mennonite. In fact, we keep on writing new confessions, or changing the old ones and trying to contextualize our beliefs.

So, why then is the Credo the high point of all music for me? There are two glorious moments in it. The first section is set up by the text "and was crucified also for us under Pontius Pilate. He suffered, died, and was buried." The music itself seems to die. This is word painting at its best, sounding almost like an old record player at half speed, a hand grabbing the vinyl, forcibly slowing it down while the sound hollowly dies. I'm drawn emotionally into an agony of ending, and Jesus' life and voice are silenced.

Then the resurrection rips open the silence. The trumpets, drums, and voices burst out a surprised but exuberant exclamation: "And the third day he arose again, according the to Scriptures." Nothing can stop the sound or the exultation or, often, my tears.

The Taflemusik Orchestra and Choir continue the Credo: "I confess one baptism for the remission of sins." Again the music sinks into the depths of anguish and solitude. Again the trumpets, drums, and voices break the chains of death. "And I look for the resurrection of the dead, and the life of the world to come. Amen." My soul runs, dances, soars. Lydia nudges me to contain myself.

Deep within I'm shouting amen to both the music and the message. I believe that the crucifixion and resurrection of Jesus are at the heart of the way God works in the world and in my life. The crucifixion proclaims that Jesus will choose to suffer and to die rather than use violence to save himself or to bring about God's kingdom. Love, not violence, is God's way. The resurrection proclaims that such profound love cannot be forever killed, that it triumphs, which means that my understanding of peace is rooted centrally in this Jesus story of crucifixion and resurrection, in this "we believe" part of the Catholic Mass. That is what gives the impetus and power to following Jesus and his way of love and of peace.

This love informs, in a very foundational way, how I understand pastoral ministry. Pastoral ministry has to be rooted in love, compassion, invitation, relationships, and empowering other people. It can't include coercion, abuse of power, domination, or threats of "hell fire." Jesus' way of peace and love, informed by the crucifixion and resurrection, is at the heart of how I understand all work as a follower of this Jesus. Much of the time I don't manage to work this way, but that is my commitment.

Mendelssohn

On Saturday evening and Sunday afternoon, the Pax Christi Chorale with full orchestra presented the oratorio *Saint Paul*, written by twenty-five-year-old Felix Mendelssohn. This time I sang bass instead of "conducting."

The Pax Christi Chorale is an inter-Mennonite choir in the greater Toronto area, conceived twenty years ago to give voice to a long and rich musical heritage. We have drawn many fine singers from other traditions into our eighty-voice chorale. Both our repertoire and our musicality are growing under the conducting of Stephanie Martin. I was a founding singer in the choir and have enjoyed singing both well-known choral works and a lot of stuff new to my ears.

Forty-five years ago I cut my singing teeth on *Saint Paul* at Canadian Mennonite Bible College. It was the first oratorio I ever sang as a squeaky, fledgling, nineteen-year-old baritone. The emotions of that experience come back to me now, partly because my oldest brother Leonard was one of the bass soloists then. I envied his ease of voice and his ease with notes.

The notes come easier for me now; age has taken some of the squeak out of my voice, though age may also have added an unwelcome wobble or two. Now I can pay more attention to the text, the story, and the emotional power of this oratorio, which sometimes awkwardly straddles baroque flourishes and romantic noise.

I had neither sung nor heard a live performance of *Saint Paul* since singing it forty-five years ago, and I wonder why. Is the music not deemed strong enough, not comparable to the great works of Bach and Handel and Mozart? Is it too risky to mount a production, which takes great musical resources for an unknown work that may not draw an audience?

The work is dramatic to a fault. The choir alternates between screaming, "Stone him, stone him" (Paul, that is), and singing exquisitely tender chorales, such as the response to the stoning of Stephen:

> To Thee, O Lord, I yield my spirit
> Who break'st, in love, this mortal chain.
> My life I but from Thee inherit,
> And death becomes my chiefest gain.
> In thee I live, in Thee I die,
> Content, for Thou art ever nigh.

Gorgeous melodies abound between the dramatic outbursts. One of the choruses that I recognize instantly is this:

> How lovely are the messengers that preach us the gospel
> of peace!
> To all the nations is gone forth the sound of their words,
> throughout all the lands their glad tidings!

The melody is imprinted on my brain. So is the memory of those college years when I was trying to sort out my own theology of peace. I'd grown up knowing that as Mennonites we were pacifists and wouldn't go to war. But the reasons for this had never been explained to me. Or, if they had been, I hadn't understood them. There seemed so many ambiguities and contradictions in trying to think about peace in a postwar world. There were so many stories of war and violence in the Old Testament.

Singing "How lovely are the messengers that preach us the gospel of peace" during a time of personal struggling with my pacifist heritage was a moment of clarity in an otherwise cloudy picture.

Mendelssohn didn't elaborate this text at all; he gave it neither context nor application. He just gave it an enduring melody.

I despair that the gospel of peace is today seldom sung or proclaimed, and that the sound most nations hear from the Christian West is war anthems.

Britten

War Requiem by Benjamin Britten is more impassioned in its plea for peace and much more hands-on in its descriptions of the battlefield. Britten used as libretto the stunning poetry of Wilfred Owen. Two soldiers sing,

> Out there, we've walked quite friendly up to death;
> Sat down and eaten with him, cool and bland,
> Pardoned his spilling mess-tins in our hand.
> We've sniffed the green thick odour of his breath.

I am intrigued by what Owen does with the story of Abraham's sacrifice of his son Isaac. He begins:

> So Abram arose, and clave the wood, and went,
> And took the fire with him, and a knife.
> And as they sojourned both of them together,
> Isaac the first-born spake and said, "My Father.
> Behold the preparations, fire and iron,
> but where the lamb for this burnt offering?"
> Then Abram bound the youth with belts and straps.
> And builded parapets and trenches there.
> And stretched forth the knife to slay his son,
> When lo! An angel called him out of heaven,
> Saying, "Lay not thy hand upon the lad.
> Neither do anything to him. Behold."

But then Owen twists the ending of this biblical story. What if? What if Abraham had struck his son?

> A ram, caught in a thicket by its horns,
> Offer the Ram of Pride instead of him.
> But the old man would not so, but slew his son—
> And half the seed of Europe, one by one.

Abram had a good life there in Ur of the Chaldeans, a great Mesopotamian city. It was a cultural center of the ancient world, like modern New York or London or Toronto. Ur was a great religious city. The moon god was its primary deity, and Abram was a decent moon-god-fearing young man. The moon god, like most gods, sometimes required child sacrifice. It was not uncommon to kill your firstborn on one kind of altar or another. (Our modern society does that too of course. Children are sacrificed to various kinds of violence all the time, but we call it by different names: child poverty, abuse, child labor, child soldiers, collateral damage, and so on.)

Abram's father, Terah, decided to pull up roots with his family and head for the sticks somewhere. No protest allowed. The family got as far as Haran and settled there. Haran was certainly no Ur, but one could imagine worse.

But one day out of the blue an unknown God called Abram, saying, "Go from your country and your kindred and your father's house to the land that I will show you. I will make of you a great nation" (Genesis 12:1-2). The long, painful, ambiguous, and often contradictory odyssey to discover what this new Lord God wanted of him had begun. Though it turned his whole life upside down, Abram went. One of the big questions was whether he would cling to the old moon god myth of sacrificial violence.

Abram started off well. When conflict erupted with his nephew Lot, who claimed the best land for himself, Abram became the peacemaker. He let Lot choose whichever land he wanted, and of course Lot chose the prime real estate near the cities of the plain, right next to Sodom. Abram had to be content with the rockier, hillier land farther away (see Genesis 13:8-13).

In the next story Abram became a warrior. In a rebellion in Sodom, Abraham's self-serving nephew Lot was captured, with all his goods taken away as booty. Abram quickly raised an army of 313 soldiers, routed the enemy, and rescued his dear nephew (see Genesis 14:12-16).

Soon the issue of violence would take a very family-centered focus. Abram's wife, Sarai, was barren. Without children, life was empty. They accepted the normal custom of the time and did what everyone else did: Sarai gave her slave girl Hagar to her husband; she would claim the child as her own (see Genesis 16:1-3).

Hagar became pregnant and everything seemed to be working out according to plan—except that Sarai grew jealous of her slave. So jealous that she drove Hagar into the desert to die. Abram did nothing to stop her and so contributed to the family violence; he was ready to sacrifice his second wife and her soon-to-be born son to Sarai's jealousy. Hagar and her son Ishmael would survive, but no thanks to Abram.

Then a miracle happened. Sarai became pregnant and gave birth to a son, Isaac. But one day, Abraham, going by the new name God had given him, hears God's voice, which commands him to take Isaac and prepare to sacrifice him. We who read this story today are dumbfounded, dismayed, ready to reject any god who dares require child sacrifice. For Abraham it was a familiar voice. The gods often demanded such sacrifice. It was time. The lot had fallen on him. What could he do? This miracle child of their old age would be offered a knife through the heart. But at the last moment, with Isaac bound to the altar awaiting the down stroke of Abraham's knife, a voice said no, the child is not to be sacrificed.

The astounding thing to the first hearers of the story, I think, would not have been that a god would require the death of a child. That was normal. It was that this God said no. How strange for this God to say that this child (and every child) is too precious to ever be wounded or damaged or abused or killed—and especially not with religious sanction. Especially not for the sake of some supposed religious gain of adults.

The voice said, "Do not lay your hand upon the boy, or do anything to him; for now I know that you fear God" (Genesis 22:12). This story has been interpreted as a test of Abraham's faith. Will his faith extend to killing his own son? I read this story much more as a rejection of child sacrifice. I read it as a momentous change of religious ethos. No, Yahweh does not require a child to die to somehow pay for a parent's sin.

A direction is set already in Genesis, a direction away from violence, away from treating children as expendable. It is a direction toward peace. Many readers of the Bible see a great dichotomy between the Old and the New Testaments. In the Old Testament God is seen as a God of war, angry and judgmental. Meanwhile the New Testament pictures a gentler, more loving God. That characterization is far too simplistic.

Abraham left the mountain with his son and with an emerging picture of what his God expected of him. He was still not a full-fledged pacifist—far from it. His family would have many more dysfunctional moments. A pacifist conviction doesn't easily grow out of the first books of our Bible, with its many stories of war and of killing. But I think a direction is set, a trajectory, and it is clear from this story that child sacrifice is not the will of God.

Oops! I used the word *trajectory*, which sounds a bit too militaristic for reflections on peace. I know the word from my hunting days. The word projectile has the same root—projectile as in bullet. Trajectory is the path a bullet takes when fired from a gun. If you have a small-caliber gun, like a .22 caliber rifle, and if the target is distant, you have to aim above what you are trying to hit, letting the bullet travel in an arc. If you guess the right trajectory, you might hit the target after all.

I grew up with guns in my hands, much to the dismay of my father. One day I was hunting pheasants with my .22, which is a rather stupid thing to do. It's hard enough to hit a flying pheasant with a shotgun, which spreads buckshot in a wide net. I flushed out a pheasant, and though I was vaguely aware of a herd of our neighbor's cattle in the distance, I took quick aim and fired anyway. I missed the pheasant, but suddenly a neighbor's cow a quarter-mile away bolted and raced across the field for dear life. I had scored a bull's-eye—or maybe a cow's hindquarter—because I hadn't calculated the trajectory. I don't think the wound was severe, but since the cow never stopped running, I couldn't investigate further. I do think there is a trajectory in the direction of peace that one can trace through the Old Testament, culminating in a peace bull's-eye in the New Testament.

But maybe I should use less violent language. How about the word thread? There is a strong peace thread that weaves its way through the biblical material, becoming stronger, more colorful, and more central as Jesus completes the tapestry.

There are many threads in Abraham's story, some of peace and some of war. But why in his poem "The Parable of the Old Man and the Young" does Owen change the ending of the story of the sacrifice of Isaac? Why does he have the old man slaying his son, and with him half the seed of Europe one by one?

Maybe because that is the reality of war. The reality of war is that fathers—politicians—send their sons—soldiers—to do the actual killing and to be killed. Yahweh does not demand it of Abraham, but our gods continue to demand it of us. Or so say our politician high priests.

At the conclusion of *War Requiem* the tenor soloist sings,

> The scribes of all the people shove
> And bawl allegiance to the state.
> But they who love the greater love
> Lay down their life, they do not hate.

Hostages for Peace

In 2005 and 2006, Christian Peacemaker Teams (CPT) gained a great deal of public attention when four of their workers were taken hostage in Iraq. The execution of Tom Fox and the rescue of Harmeet Singh Sooden, James Loney, and Norman Kember unleashed an important public debate about the wisdom of the team's risk-taking peace work in Iraq and other places of violence around the world. Should peace activists put their lives in danger in an attempt to "get in the way" of people killing each other? *War Requiem* does anticipate such a possibility.

> But they who love the greater love
> Lay down their life, they do not hate.

Soldiers are expected to put their lives at risk while trying to kill the enemy. That's what soldiers do. So why is it so unreasonable and "naive" for people committed to peace also to put their lives at risk for what they passionately believe in? The four who were held hostage knew the risks they were taking and were willing to accept that danger.

Doug Pritchard, co-director of CPT, is a member of our congregation. He carried an enormous weight of responsibility during the hostage ordeal. We heard almost daily updates, and we prayed as a congregation for Doug and the hostages every Sunday.

The rescue of the hostages is filled with irony. They were in Iraq as peacemakers, their peace convictions shaped by their Christian faith. They publicly stated that the coalition forces should not be in Iraq. They had forged friendships with many Muslim leaders. Yet they were taken hostage by a Muslim group, and they were rescued by coalition forces that they had critiqued. These forces had been sent to Iraq by a Christian president and a Christian prime minister.

It boggles the mind. Perhaps the thread of peace will always be filled with contradictions, ambiguities, and ironies.

A Personal Confession

I pride myself on being able to live peaceably with most people. I'm committed to making peace in personal relationships. That is a part of how I understand Jesus' way of peace. But recently my wife and I were total failures in an attempt to make peace with our basement tenants.

We are reluctant landlords at best. But buying a second house felt like the right thing to do to provide housing for family members in Toronto. To make it affordable for them and to pay for part of the mortgage, we rented out a basement apartment. Shortly after the renter moved in, her boyfriend moved in with her. She didn't pay her rent, and she damaged the apartment. We tried discussion, negotiation, and setting clear deadlines, boundaries, and expectations. Then we tried eviction, and she tried suing us, but her suit was thrown out of court. We finally reached an unhappily mediated settlement, and she left the apartment and some months of unpaid rent.

We've always seen ourselves as reasonable people who can get along with almost everybody. But our efforts to make peace failed, and we evicted our tenants. When they finally left, we were relieved but took no joy from it. It had been a relationship that we didn't know how to mend. We could not control their response to our efforts at peacemaking.

It's sobering to be an advocate for Christian pacifism when I feel I'm a failure at making peace with a tenant. Maybe I need to be reminded again that the way of peace is not guaranteed to work, that the world is messy and violent and not necessarily amenable to good-hearted Christian peacemakers.

Healing the Enemy

While most people find only the war strands in the Old Testament stories, I delight in discovering peace strands that are newly visible to me. The story of Naaman from 2 Kings I knew well from childhood, but it never touched my imagination then.

Naaman was the commander of the Aramean—that is, Syrian—army. He was Israel's enemy number one. The Arameans were a brutal, big-bully power that kept molesting Israel. They raided with impunity, burning, looting, enslaving Israel's finest young men and women, and laughing at their "weak" God, Yahweh, who couldn't seem to protect them.

Naaman and his king believed that they were autonomous because of their great power, that they could make their own rules and were accountable to no one. They ruled their own people with an exploitive social policy and forged a cruel foreign policy, especially against weakling Israel. They were insane with power.

Naaman's path was straight, hard, cruel, carefully scripted, and dedicated to absolute control of every variable except one. Naaman had leprosy, and all his power could not subdue it. But even leprosy didn't quell his arrogance or harshness. As his body wasted away uncontrollably, he was driven to exert greater control of those things and people in his power. He led raid after raid into Israel. He took a young girl captive and made her a slave for his wife. This slave isn't given a name in this story; slaves didn't need names. But this nameless girl did not lose her decency and compassion, despite being forcibly captured. She held on to the freedom of her faith.

"I know what Naaman should do," she told her new mistress with innocent compassion. "We have a prophet in Israel, a true man of God. If my lord would go there, this prophet would surely heal him" (see 2 Kings 5). Naaman's wife (she isn't named either; maybe commanders' wives also weren't important enough) took this faint ray of hope to her husband. He took it to his king, who sent him with an official delegation to the king of Israel, replete with loads of gold and silver and gifts and documents—and just enough hinted threats to remind Israel who controlled the levers of power. It was humiliating to need something that only a lesser power could deliver, so a show of arrogance and wealth was in order.

The king of Israel received Naaman's glitzy entourage but was cowed by them. "He tore his clothes and said, 'Am I God, to give death or life, that this man sends word to me to cure a man with leprosy? Just look and see how he is trying to pick a quarrel with me'" (2 Kings 5:7). The king breathed the same power madness as did the king of Aram. In it he smelled his own doom and was terrified.

Elisha the prophet breathed different air. He knew that the various kings and their self-importance had limited power. He was attuned to a far greater power, to Yahweh, who held the mightiest nations to account.

"Send Naaman to me," said Elisha simply, unimpressed with kings and commanders and enough gold to pave the road to Jerusalem. When Naaman arrived, only Elisha's servant met him, and with a bizarre message. The servant told Naaman to wash seven times in the small, dirty Jordan River. This would cleanse him of his leprosy. How utterly humiliating!

> But Naaman became angry and went away, saying, "I thought that for me he would surely come out, and stand and call on the name of the Lord his God, and would wave his hand over the spot, and cure the leprosy! Are not Abana and Pharpar, the rivers of Damascus, better than all the waters of Israel? Could I not wash in them, and be clean?" He turned and went away in a rage. (5:11-12)

What a picture! What a story! A commander was reduced to spluttering rage because he couldn't demand healing on his own terms. The rivers back home were thought to have healing powers. They were grander and cleaner by far than the Jordan. His servants, though, saw everything more clearly. Power and the world look different from the vantage point of a servant.

They ask, "If the prophet had commanded you to do something really difficult, wouldn't you have done it?" (verse 13). Controlling his simmering, helpless rage, Naaman reluctantly went down into the Jordan and immersed himself the required seven times. He emerged with "his flesh restored like the flesh of a young boy, and he was clean" (verse 14).

Healed, humbled, but not yet released from his mindset of rank and power, Naaman finally met the prophet. He and all his company came and stood before this solitary man of God, and he said, "Now I know that there is no God in all the earth except in Israel" (verse 15). This was the great moment of the story. The climax was not the healing but Naaman's confession that there is no God in all the earth except Yahweh. The powerful Syrian commander named the God of his enemy as the only true God. He had been healed by his enemy.

Feeding the Enemy

In another story in 2 Kings, Ben-hadad was frustrated. He had decided to ambush the king of Israel and take control of his people and wealth. But each time he planned an ambush, he was thwarted. The king somehow always escaped. Ben-hadad suspected spies within his own court, but his servants said it was probably the prophet Elisha who somehow divined the plan and warned his king.

So a great army was dispatched to capture Elisha. It surrounded the little town of Dothan where Elisha was staying. But he was not perturbed when he saw the great enemy army closing in on him. He prayed to the Lord, "Strike this army, please, with blindness." Every enemy soldier was struck blind, and Elisha led the enemy into the capital city of Samaria, where they were at the mercy of the Israelite army. There, weaponless, defenseless, and surrounded, they received their sight back and realized that they are doomed.

The king of Israel exulted, "Shall I kill them? Shall I kill them?"

"No!" says Elisha. "You shall not kill them. You shall feed them. You shall prepare a great banquet for them and send them on their way." And that is what they did.

The editor's final comment on this story is, "And the Arameans no longer came raiding into the land of Israel" (see 2 Kings 6).

Feed your enemy instead of killing them and you make a genuine peace. You turn enemies into friends. The apostle Paul picked up this theme in Romans 12: "If your enemies are hungry, feed them; if they are thirsty, give them something to drink" (verse 20, quoting Proverbs 25:21).

I marvel at these two stories, told out of the arena of power, lust, and brutal oppression. Two strands—heal the enemy and feed the enemy—become woven into a peace tapestry.

I Could Have Cursed God

Peace is not easily won, not even inner peace, and murder is not easily forgotten.

My father-in-law, Rev. C. K. Neufeld, told us a story at his fiftieth wedding celebration. He hadn't meant to, but it just poured out of him. He just wanted to do some sharing of his background before he met his wife of fifty years. He never got that far. He got stuck in Russia instead.

My father-in-law was a lay preacher in a Mennonite church, one of four or five who took turns interpreting the Scriptures to the congregation. Occasionally he was asked to serve as lead preacher. During those times of leading the congregation, he received a stipend. Other than that, he was never paid for his role. He earned his living as a fruit and egg farmer.

Dad was a teenager in the Ukraine when the Russian Revolution raced like a tsunami through the idyllic existence of the Mennonite colonies there. These Mennonites of Dutch background had come to Russia from Prussia in the 1780's. They had been invited by Catherine the Great of Russia to move to the Ukraine to help fill vast, empty farmland. There they established a prosperous and independent life with little outside interference by the Russian state.

But then came the Russian Revolution. In the civil war that followed, both the White Army and the Red Army often used Mennonite villages as battlegrounds or at least as resting and looting place between battles. Worse were the large groups of bandits intent on looting, rape, and mayhem. Whole armies of anarchist bandits took advantage of the power vacuum of civil war to wreak their havoc. One such group came to the Neufeld farm. Lydia's grandfather went into the yard to investigate the commotion, and they immediately shot him. He died a day later.

We'd heard that story before. We could only imagine the turmoil it caused Dad, because he told only the bare story. He never talked about his emotions. Dad and the rest of the family soon emigrated to Canada, where he preached an evangelical gospel often filled with challenges to be committed to Jesus' way of peace.

But in this telling at the big anniversary celebration, suddenly the emotions of losing his father through that murder more than fifty years earlier began spilling out. He told of witnessing his father's murder. His voice got louder, his physical movements more agitated.

Finally he acknowledged, "I could have cursed God in his face."

He told us that he still shudders when he remembers his feelings then. But he also told us how, through that testing, he had eventually committed himself "to be held by divine love . . . to let God hold me in his bosom." He had made a fresh vow to "let God use me as an instrument of his peace and of his love." Dad's commitment to peace was hard won.

A Wrong Not Forgiven

Conflicts happen among leaders in the church too, even in so-called peace churches. Once my father-in-law was deeply embroiled in one that threatened to split the church apart. Angry words, accusations, and suspicions became loudly public. But at one point the leaders made an effort to resolve their conflicts and make peace. They gathered with their spouses (who so often feel the hurt as much or more than those shouting at each other) and spoke words of confession and forgiveness to each other. My mother-in-law participated and said the words, "Yes, I forgive you."

When Mom and Dad returned home from the meeting, Mom turned to Dad and said, "We have to go back."

"What do you mean, we have to go back?"

"I haven't really forgiven him in my heart. I said the words, but I didn't mean them. We have to go back."

Mom and Dad got right back into their car and drove to the home of the minister with whom they were most angry. There Mom confessed that her forgiveness had not been real but had only been nice words.

Something deep and powerful happened that evening. The two

couples genuinely forgave each other and became fast friends for life.

Handel

I love a good fugue. A fugue is very different from our traditional four-part-harmony hymn, which I love too. The name derives from the Latin word *fuga*, which means "flight." The melody takes flight; it's not tied to earth anymore. Or maybe the flight is the tune passing back and forth between flying songbirds represented by voice parts.

A fugue begins with one melody line sung or played by one voice or instrument. That melody states a theme that is passed on to another singer or player. Then a second melody line is introduced and developed. The first and second theme will be restated over and over, often with variations. But you always recognize the tune. Occasionally all the voice or instrumental parts come together in a rousing climax.

George Frideric Handel built most of the choruses in *The Messiah* on a fugal structure. Take "For unto us a child is born" as an example. The sopranos make the first statement of theme: "For unto us a child is born, unto us, a son is given." They then hand the tune off to the tenors, while they continue with a very light run over top of it. The tenors sing the theme, then hand it over to the altos, who pass it on to the basses. The basses surprise everyone by not quite finishing the theme before they jump right to their run. Basses are often accused of being a bit behind the beat, so maybe this is their way of catching up again. Meanwhile, the tenors find another theme, a second statement: "And the government shall be upon his shoulders and his name shall be called." By this time the sopranos, altos, and basses have hurried to catch up, and all come together in a glorious, harmonic "Wonderful, Counselor, the Mighty God, the Everlasting Father, the Prince of Peace."

Throughout the Scriptures, the theme of peace is played like a great fugue. There are opposing themes and counter melodies aplenty, of course, especially in the Old Testament. Visions of violence and war are spun out, and there is some competition between the violence themes and the peace themes; sometimes it's not clear which one is going to be given the most beautiful melody and will be sung the most.

Many people are convinced that the peace theme is too weak a melody line for real life. Fugues built on violence get more attention. The myth of redemptive violence has always been one of the greatest of all religious myths; it's given the most powerful media melodies. It sings that the only effective way to deal with evil is on its own terms, to be even more violent and more evil than your enemies are.

By the time Isaiah came along, it was becoming clear that God is conducting the peace fugue, not the violence fugue. God gives peace the great melodies and their variations bursting out with creative imagination, and occasionally God brings the choir together in great climactic moments when everyone is singing together in grand harmony. But always there are competing melodies trying to overpower it.

Isaiah, Weaver of Peace Melodies

Isaiah was a master at building a long, complex, and beautiful fugue on the theme of peace. In chapter 2, he stated his grand vision for peace, the opening melody line to be repeated throughout the book. Chapter 2 is the great cosmic picture that reveals the will of God for all nations: "He shall judge between the nations, and shall arbitrate for many peoples; they shall beat their swords into plowshares, and their spears into pruning hooks; nation shall not lift up sword against nation, neither shall they learn war any more" (verse 4). It's a fantastic vision and a stunning melody.

In chapter 9 Isaiah stated a second melody line, this one proclaiming how this vision will be achieved and who will sing the melody throughout the world: "For a child has been born to us, a son given to us; authority rests upon his shoulders; and he is named Wonderful Counselor, Mighty God, Everlasting Father, Prince of Peace. His authority shall grow continually, and there shall be endless peace for the throne of David and his kingdom" (verses 6-7).

So melody 1 is the grand vision: peace instead of war. Melody 2 is the good news that a child to be born will be the one singing it above the noise of war. But between these two melodies will be a lot of dissonance and tension that is not necessarily resolved by a satis-fying cadence. King Ahaz will not buy into Isaiah's vision; he will not sign up to sing in the choir. He is into a different kind of music alto-gether—the heavy amplification of war drumming. Isaiah will need to live out a parable to try to unplug Ahaz's amplifiers.

In the middle of the eight century BC, Ahaz was king of Judah during chaotic, even desperate, times. He and his people were ter-rified. The narrator writes, "The heart of Ahaz and the heart of the people shook as the trees of the forest shake before the wind" (7:2). Why? There were enemies everywhere they looked—big ene-mies with big weapons.

It was so stupid, really. Not long before, King Rehoboam had so foolishly divided the country. He had listened to his young, hot-headed advisers rather than to the older, wiser sages and had insti-gated a harsh, dictatorial rule. The rebellion that followed divided the country in two. Now these two parts, Israel and Judah, were enemies. The northern kingdom of Israel wanted to invade Judah to the south and really teach her a lesson. To do this, Israel had formed a military alliance with Syria, and the two together were very strong.

Even further north loomed Assyria, lusting for world domina-tion and flexing its huge muscles. No wonder Ahaz's heart was shaking like a tree in the forest in a windstorm. What was the poor king to do? He was running hard to keep up with everything, and there were enemies behind every tree.

In terror Ahaz strategized like kings do. "Maybe," he reasoned, "if I make a treaty with Assyria, she will keep Israel and Syria in check." So Ahaz cozied up to Assyria, paid some tribute, imported some Assyrian gods and their priests, and generally bent over back-ward to placate the foreign giant and win its benevolence. Yes, it meant watering down faith and commitments to Yahweh, but these were desperate times, and the king had to be realistic and logical and responsible. Didn't he?

Enter Isaiah the prophet, who just happened to be carrying a baby in his arms. "Well, Isaiah, how nice to see you," said Ahaz, as polite a lie as he knew how to give. He wasn't at all pleased to see the prophet. "How have you been while I was visiting my friend

Tiglath-pileser, ruler of Assyria, and securing peace? Great treaty, don't you think?"

"I've been doing very well, thank you," Isaiah replied. "Look, my lord, while you were away my wife had a baby. Here, see, isn't he cute?"

"Of course he's cute. All babies are cute, Isaiah. What did you call him at the naming?"

"We call him Shear-jashub. As you know, my lord King Ahaz, that means, 'a few will come back.'"

By this time Ahaz was beginning to suspect something deeply disconcerting coming from his crazy prophet. "Why would you call him 'a few will come back,' Isaiah?"

"Well, king, you have not trusted the God of your forefathers. You have made a treaty with a ruthless man. You have made a covenant with death, and if you don't trust in Yahweh instead, Assyria will run over our country like a scythe, and you and the rest of your secure upper class will be carted off and only a few will come back. But it doesn't need to be that way. There is still time for you to sing a peace melody instead." (See Isaiah 7:3ff.)

The next time Isaiah visits Ahaz he is not carrying a baby, which must have pleased Ahaz. He has had enough of cooing billboards. But Isaiah tells of a baby to be born, who will be named Emmanuel—God with us (see Isaiah 7:10-14). Herein would lie great hope, if only Ahaz could see it. But he can't.

Isaiah will come once more to his king, this time again with a baby. This son was called Ma'her-shal'al-hash-baz. The name means "quick loot, fast plunder" (Isaiah 8:3). "You will lose everything if you keep on singing your peace-through-arms-and-alliances song, Ahaz," Isaiah said. "You keep on memorizing the wrong tune."

There will be another message from the Lord, this one probably sung to the whole people. It is a magnificent new melody:

> The people who walked in darkness have seen a great light.
> . . . For a child has been born for us, a son given to us;
> authority rests upon his shoulders; and he is named
> Wonderful Counselor, Mighty God, Everlasting Father,
> Prince of Peace. His authority shall grow continually, and
> there shall be endless peace for the throne of David and his

kingdom. He will establish and uphold it with justice and
with righteousness. (9:2, 6-7)

Poor Ahaz. His situation was getting more desperate every day.
He was dealing with world powers and great armies and ruthless
schemers. All Isaiah could do was sing a song about a baby born.
Who knew who that baby even was? Was it another of Isaiah's
sons? This baby was fixated on peace through justice and righteousness. How would that fight Israel's or Syria's armies? Ahaz
never did join the peace choir or sing the peace fugue. In the end he
suffered all the consequences Isaiah had named.

Seven hundred years later, another baby was born. Whether this
was the child Isaiah had announced to Ahaz is not clear. But this
baby would fulfill Isaiah's vision of the "God with us," who would
become the Prince of Peace.

Seven hundred years after Isaiah challenged Ahaz to stop trusting in his Machiavellian alliances and trust a child for salvation
instead, Judah was again in crisis. Rome was now the world power,
and Israel was under its thumb. Again fear and gloom inhabited
every corner. Every Jew desperately longed for the Messiah to rescue them. There was some confusion about who the Messiah
would be and how he would go about saving his people. Most said
the Messiah would be a warrior who would drive out the hated
Romans and restore peace through war.

Instead, God again sent a baby. Why does God keep sending
babies when what you really need is a heroic man? A baby!
Helpless. Powerless. All it can do is love, be loved, and sing.

The great peace fugue had a new singer and a new melody. The
voice was still a child's, but thirty years later he would become the
conductor of the peace choir and the composer in residence, adding
ever new variations to the fugue: "Blessed are the peacemakers."
"Love even your enemies." "Peter, put away your sword." "Father,
forgive them, for they know not what they do."

But there were so many more compelling songs, then as now,
and most refused to sing along with Jesus. In fact, the peace fugue
sounded so threatening to the powers that Jesus had to be killed to
silence the song.

How could the silencers have known that a resurrection would elevate the song and that the martyrs would sing it into eternity. But even the followers of Jesus a few centuries later tired of the peace song. They declared it obsolete, naive, surely intended for another time, and they lustily added their voices to a hymn dedicated to the myth of redemptive violence. "In the name of Christ, conquer," proclaimed Emperor Constantine, after declaring Christianity the state religion of the Roman Empire in the fourth century. Now Christ would serve the political and military goals of expansion. Jesus faded into irrelevance and obscurity, while this "in the name of Christ, conquer" hymn seems still to be the main song of a supposedly Christian West today.

Another Betrayal

This story slips through my defenses. Suddenly it's there, and I relive my sense of betrayal and my feeling of anguish. It is an unwanted interruption in my writing journey through peace. But it was John Howard Yoder who most clearly shaped my own peace theology. It was he who most articulately deconstructed the Christianization of the church in the fourth century and reconstructed for me a viable and plausible peace theology based on the Jesus of the Gospels.

Yoder was my teacher at Associated Mennonite Biblical Seminary in Elkhart, Indiana, between 1968 and 1971. My fellow students and I thrived in his courses. His book *The Politics of Jesus* (Eerdmans, 1972) and the lectures we heard leading up to its publication made a powerful impact on me and many others. Yoder articulated for us a way of reading the story of Jesus to see its enormous social and political impact. His was a radical reading that challenged Christians who had abandoned Jesus' peace teachings as irrelevant and unrealistic, and us pacifists (especially Mennonites) who quietly and personally believed in nonviolence but didn't apply the teachings of Jesus to our political context. I was in awe of this seminary professor.

Years later, rumors emerged that Yoder had sexually abused some of his female students. Then I heard directly from a colleague of mine that Yoder had abused her. I was devastated. Yoder had taught me that an understanding of peace built on Jesus' framework rejects all forms of violence, coercion, and abuse. Now I'd learned that he'd violated this eloquently stated theology. He'd violated some female students. He had violated a friend of mine.

Does the theology collapse with those violations? Is there a flaw in this system of thought or in his reading of Jesus? Or is the flaw deep inside the teacher? Were theology and life somehow divided from each other, a chasm between what he believed and taught and how he lived his relationships? Is the flaw the normal sinfulness of all us human creatures?

I suppose gaining power always brings with it huge temptations to abuse that power, even when your belief structure warns against that temptation. Certainly Yoder had gained enormous power from his brilliance and international reputation.

Yoder did finally submit to discipline from his congregation and from the seminary. He agreed to quietly leave his teaching position. His home church processed the charges against him, tried to hold him accountable, and tried to establish appropriate boundaries for him.

This story of betrayal has also impacted me because I've had to offer pastoral care to a number of persons who were sexually and physically abused. I've heard many stories of pain and despair. The devastation of abuse goes so deep. Healing from betrayal is such a long, complex, and painful journey. So it hit me particularly hard when a revered teacher, one committed to peace and nonviolence, acted violently.

My anguish, reawakened now as I write this, reminds me that mess and chaos and sin are never far away, including in the lives of committed pacifists. Contradictions and ambiguities abound, perhaps in our theology and surely in the living out of our faith.

Did the Father Sacrifice the Son?

I wonder how the Jesus of the Gospels was transformed into the conquering Christ of the Constantinian church. Did the early church gradually change its understanding of the meaning of Jesus' crucifixion? I'm in deep waters here, over my head in stuff in which only the foolhardy submerge themselves. But I wonder if Abraham's almost-sacrifice of Isaac can help me sort this one out.

I wonder if Benjamin Britten's *War Requiem* and its libretto of the poetry of Wilfred Owen offers a particular insight here.

In the Genesis story of the almost-sacrifice of Isaac, the voice at the end says, "Do not lay your hand upon the boy." Child sacrifice was not what God wanted or demanded. But we have interpreted the crucifixion story as God the Father demanding the sacrificial death of the son Jesus. This "once and for all" sacrifice of this sinless human frees us from our sins. The father needed the son to be sacrificed in order to fulfill his plan of salvation for us humans. In fact, that was the plan from the beginning: Jesus was sent to earth in order to be crucified.

But this would mean that all focus is placed on the sacrificial death of Jesus. No longer is it as important that Jesus came to earth as the incarnation of God to show us a fuller and clearer picture of who God is. Want to know what God is like? Look at Jesus. No longer is it important that the message of Isaiah that the son to be born would be God with us. No longer is Jesus' teaching of loving even our enemies important, nor is his life of healing and loving and forgiving and empowering people. Not even the resurrection is essential anymore. What is important is that Jesus fulfilled his life by being crucified as was planned by God the Father. Child sacrifice is the thing.

Maybe Wilfred Owen read into the Abraham story the Christian story: "But the old man would not so, but slew his son / And half the seed of Europe, one by one."

I believe that Jesus died for my sins. But if that is the most important thing to believe, then I can in the end ignore the deeper meaning of the incarnation. I can ignore the lessons of Jesus' life, his teachings about love and peace, especially the Sermon on the Mount (Matthew 5–7). Then I can easily embrace the "in the name of Christ, conquer" slogan, and I can go deal with my enemies in the way of the world, with violence. The Christian church over the centuries has been ingenious in finding ways to avoid taking the life and teaching of Jesus seriously when it comes to participating in violence, coercion, and war. And this ingenuity may be rooted in a narrow theology of salvation in which Jesus was destined for sacrifice.

Owen points in a different direction.

> The scribes of all the people shove
> And bawl allegiance to the state.
> But they who love the greater love
> Lay down their life, they do not hate.

Is that not what Jesus did? With greater love he laid down his life. But he did it with free choice, not because it was demanded of him by his Father, or because it was predestined as the only way to save us wretched humans, or because his sacrifice somehow appeased a vengeful and angry Father God, but because love saw no other way.

Most compelling to me is that Jesus chose to die rather than kill. He chose to love his enemies to the end rather than to bring down his legions of angels to destroy them. In choosing to die rather than kill, he demonstrated the ultimate kind of loving—God's kind.

Jesus' resurrection is the ultimate vindication of his choice to reject violence as the answer to evil. It is the ultimate statement that the power of love is greater than the power of evil and of violence. This love, and this resurrection, is loosed on the world as the great saving power. It is far more powerful than an enforced sacrifice that mechanically and legally removes my sinfulness.

Central to my understanding of the gospel is that Jesus' message was one of love and nonviolence. He was willing to die rather than violate this essence of who he was—and who God the Father is. Consequently the use of violence can never be justified "in the name of Christ." Nor can violence ever be justified to enforce religious beliefs.

I think that God chooses to stay in the mess of our human lives and doesn't need to get everything cleaned up right away. God doesn't act with violence or threat to force a clean and orderly life on us. Rather, God just enters our human chaos with a loving presence and with an invitation for us to do the sweeping we need to do in order for us to clear the mess. God offers only a loving and healing presence. Is that enough?

If that is enough for God, then it has to be enough for all Jesus' followers, including pastors. As a pastor I dared not abuse the power the church has given me. I needed to fulfill my calling in a way that's invitational, loving, gentle, relational. To me this is the way of peace. It meant a willingness to stay in the mess and not feel that I could quickly, neatly, and forcefully clean things up in people's lives by using my authority and power. I had to forego illusions that I am anyone's savior. That was one of my great struggles in pastoral ministry. How could I use power in a healthy way. How could I resist the temptation to abuse my power? How could I be content (and courageous enough) to simply enter into the mess with compassion and invitation and the love of God?

The Great Peace Theme

On Easter Sunday 2005, I conducted our church choir, something I seldom do because there are far better musicians than me at Toronto United Mennonite Church. But they weren't available, so I happily became the substitute. I selected a fugue, "Praise the Lord" by Handel, for one of the three anthems, though I'm aware again of an irony. This anthem came from *Judas Maccabeus*, an oratorio about the general who helped the Jewish people gain independence from the Syrians around the year 166 BC. A consummate guerilla warrior, he won battle after battle against the hated Syrians and eventually drove them out. When Jesus came along, he was compared unfavorably with this Judas. In many ways Judas epitomized the ideal messiah figure for most Jewish people. Jesus very deliberately rejected this idealization of the Messiah, championing the way of peace and love rather than violence—a polar opposite myth, as it were. Because of that he was seldom recognized as *the* Messiah.

On that Easter Sunday, our church choir sang an anthem that glorified a war hero. Only the musicologists in our congregation would have recognized that irony. But then, the church has often taken music from very unlikely sources and recrafted it for divine purposes.

"Praise the Lord" dances with joy. It has no war drums providing the beat. The altos sing the first theme in this glorious fugue: "Praise the Lord. Let songs of joy break forth." The sopranos pick up the theme, their higher notes adding to its power. The tenors and basses barge in to a full four part theme: "Shout, sing and dance and celebrate." Every voice part then goes into a running dance before coming together again for "O praise His holy name forevermore."

That was enough to help us celebrate resurrection. It was enough to help us celebrate Jesus' way of being Messiah rather than Judas Maccabeus's way.

The world will surely still be in a mess after Easter, more mess than we know what to do with. The temptation will always be to choose Judas Maccabeus, not Jesus, as our model for coping with it.

But I celebrate God's way of making peace—a way of suffering and of crucifixion and of resurrection. God, through Jesus, keeps on inviting us to join the weavers, putting new threads into the peace tapestry. This Jesus keeps on inviting new singers to join the choir singing peace fugues. We can weave and sing with hope, not despair. Resurrection happened and continues to happen.

THE AUTHOR

 Gary Harder became pastor of Toronto United Mennonite Church in 1987. He was born in Rosemary, Alberta, and grew up on a farm. He attended Mennonite schools and colleges, and holds a Doctor of Ministry degree from St. Stephen's College in Edmonton. He became a pastor in 1965, and served as a pastor in five churches over his forty-two year career. In the 1990s, he served in various Mennonite leadership positions serving on conference boards, mentoring student interns and pastors and teaching courses on church and ministry. Gary married Lydia Neufeld in 1964, and they are the parents of three children and have six grandchildren. He retired from full time pastoral ministry in 2007 but continues teaching and short-term ministry assignments.